Crash Course in Technology Planning

Recent Titles in
Libraries Unlimited Crash Course Series

Crash Course in Technology Planning

Christopher D. Brown

Crash Course

LIBRARIES
UNLIMITED™
An Imprint of ABC-CLIO, LLC
Santa Barbara, California • Denver, Colorado

Library of Congress Cataloging-in-Publication Data

Names: Brown, Christopher D., 1983– author.
Title: Crash course in technology planning / Christopher D. Brown.
Description: Santa Barbara, CA : Libraries Unlimited, [2016] | Series: Crash course |
    Includes bibliographical references and index. | Description based on print version
    record and CIP data provided by publisher; resource not viewed.
Identifiers: LCCN 2016014095 (print) | LCCN 2016002980 (ebook) |
    ISBN 9781440850615 (eBook) | ISBN 9781440850608 (pbk. : acid-free paper)
Subjects: LCSH: Libraries—Information technology—Planning. | Libraries—
    Automation—Planning. | Public libraries—Information technology—
    United States. | Public libraries—United States—Automation.
Classification: LCC Z678.9 (print) | LCC Z678.9 .B76 2016 (ebook) |
    DDC 025.00285—dc23
LC record available at http://lccn.loc.gov/2016014095

ISBN: 978-1-4408-5060-8
EISBN: 978-1-4408-5061-5

20 19 18 17 16   1 2 3 4 5

This book is also available on the World Wide Web as an eBook.
Visit www.abc-clio.com for details.

Libraries Unlimited
An Imprint of ABC-CLIO, LLC

ABC-CLIO, LLC
130 Cremona Drive, P.O. Box 1911
Santa Barbara, California 93116-1911

This book is printed on acid-free paper ∞

Manufactured in the United States of America

CONTENTS

ACKNOWLEDGMENTS

Many, many people provided assistance as I gathered the knowledge that would eventually become *Crash Course in Technology Planning*. I would like to thank my wife, Kati, for her outstanding editing and revision skills, as well as her moral support throughout this process. Diane Brown also read the first manuscript and provided excellent feedback and suggestions.

Thank you to Master Electrician Gene Van Berkum, who reviewed the chapter on electricity. A special thanks to Kyle Winward, Technology Services Librarian at Central College, for being my sounding board throughout this process and for taking the time to read a very early and very bad draft of what would eventually become this book.

Others who deserve credit here include Glenda Hunt, Director of the Adair County Public Library (Kirksville, Missouri), for her willingness to sponsor my library internship when I was still very green to the profession; Goodie Bhullar, Cindy Cotner, Rhonda Whithaus, and the entire reference team at the University of Missouri–Columbia Ellis Library for their invaluable guidance as I trained to become a professional librarian; and Dr. Thomas Kochtanek, an excellent information sciences professor, who inspired me to continue to find ways to integrate libraries and technology.

The Scenic Regional Library (Union, Missouri) and the Pella Public Library (Pella, Iowa) both played important roles as I learned and applied my trade. Finally, I want to say thank you to the staff at Libraries Unlimited for this amazing opportunity.

I dedicate this book to my family, near and far. Thanks for believing in me and this crazy idea from the very start.

CHAPTER 1

Introduction

Welcome! If you've opened this book, chances are good that you are a new IT manager in a public library and that you are the only person responsible for the IT work. You may have applied for the IT position and been politely asked (or not so politely told) that IT is now your job description or, like me, been told that IT work is just one of the many hats that you have to wear on a daily basis. Fear not! This book is written for individuals with little-to-no IT training, who have suddenly found themselves thrust into responsibility for the day-to-day IT work in a small-to-medium-sized public library or other service organization. This book is ideal for those who have multiple responsibilities; it addresses customer service as well as more technical aspects, such as networking. Even though the focus is on the public library, the information in this book could also be applied to other organizations with similar missions, such as schools and churches.

Even if you have no IT experience, this book will help you find the path to becoming an IT manager who can independently set goals and manage IT projects with ease. I will guide you toward making smart, well-reasoned IT decisions and give you a workflow to find your way through any hardware or software problem.

Though no book can completely address every possible situation that may occur, in this book I will provide you with simple, generalized templates upon which you can then build knowledge specific to your organization. For example, when this book describes a "typical" network, I acknowledge that not every single network might be set up in the same way. However, the basic understanding that I provide can still serve as a platform upon which you can learn more about your specific library's circumstances.

WHERE DO WE COME FROM?

Each of us thrust into the IT limelight has a different story with the same end: you've been made responsible for equipment and services that you may know very little about. You may be an expert at using a mouse and a keyboard, and perhaps even hooked up a computer cable once or twice, but when it comes to the inner workings of these machines or, heaven forbid, the network rack, you are in entirely foreign territory. To compound this issue, management has decided that a single person can handle the IT work for the organization, and you're it.

As the designated IT person on the staff, you may be responsible for a variety of roles. One of the most common tasks is everyday troubleshooting. You may be called upon multiple times in a single day to assist with staff and patron questions. These questions will mainly deal with how to perform various tasks on a computer, such as how to format a print job in a certain way. Other questions may deal with typical hardware and software issues, such as a patron who is having difficulty opening a file or getting his or her flash drive to work with the library computers. This book includes a guide to working with staff and a path to finding the root cause of the issue that the person is experiencing.

You will also be responsible for the troubleshooting that goes beyond simple user issues, such as the computer that will not turn on or start up correctly. In these situations, you will be called upon to diagnose the problem as either a hardware- or software-based failure and take appropriate steps to resolve it in a timely manner. This book will provide you with a road map for correcting some of these types of issues. It also covers a variety of utility programs that you can use to help when diagnosing hardware and software problems.

As an IT person, you will be called upon to maintain both the public and staff computers and other technology in the library, ensuring that software remains up-to-date and the machines themselves are running well. Through a combination of Windows and other software updates and utilities that help you optimize your computer, you'll be called upon to set up a regular schedule for maintenance so that every machine is performing at its peak. A strong maintenance program is an integral part of your job, and this book will show you some commonly used maintenance programs, as well as walk you through software and hardware updates as they are necessary.

In your role as an IT professional, you may also be called upon to manage the IT budget and procure (buy) those items for the library which seem most in line with the library's technology goals. Even if you have not worked in procurement before, this book provides an introductory guide to working with vendors, starting and completing the bidding process, including writing a request for bids, and receiving the items once they arrive at your library.

Finally, a library IT person must plan and set goals for the future. This book will walk you through the steps to creating and keeping an inventory of technology in your library. It will also give you some tips for setting goals for the future and determining the direction for the IT program in your library. Every program is unique, but this book will guide you in the process used to make your library IT service the very best that it can be.

IT work in the library is an exciting and challenging profession. It entails a wide variety of responsibilities and is constantly changing as technology emerges and evolves. It is also a role in which you will feel justly satisfied in helping to make the day of both patrons and staff a little bit better through providing them with technology and services that meet the needs of these groups. This book was written for the nonprofessional, and it is designed to get you on your feet as quickly as possible with IT work. Let's dive in.

CHAPTER 2

Set Yourself Up for Success

In this chapter, you will learn how to set yourself up for success. We begin with a tool that IT professionals use all the time: Google.

GOOGLE IS YOUR FRIEND

Born in 1998 (yes, it's really that young), Google was in the beginning just another search engine. But it quickly stood out among the pack because of its corporate culture and its amazing ability to collect and analyze search results like no one had ever seen before. Constructed around its clean, easy-to-use interface, the Google search product effectively sold itself, making the company worth billions in just a few short years.

Consider the saying, "If you've asked a question, someone has probably asked it before you." The Internet provides us with an amazing opportunity to get connected with that hive mind. Using Google as a gateway, the answers for many of your questions are just a Google search away. Need to configure a wireless router? Just Google it. Need drivers for your network card? Just Google it. Not sure why your computer is playing the first bars of Beethoven's ninth symphony whenever you turn it on? Just Google it.

You get the idea. And actually, the Google "natural language" search has become so exceptionally good that you can present your search in the form of a question if that is helpful (i.e., "How do I configure a wireless router?"). **Natural Language Search** is simply a search engine's ability to take a phrase written in the form a human being would speak and algorithmically turn that into an internal search phrase and use it to return appropriate, relevant results. Contrast natural language search with the past, where searching a database required keywords and Boolean operators, making the same search look something like this: "Wireless AND router AND configuration OR directions." You can easily see that natural language search is preferable and is a part of what has made Google such a resounding success.

My realization that I, too, could be an IT expert happened the day a local professional came in response to my call. As I looked over his shoulder to see how he solved the problem, there he was Googling the answer because he didn't know it himself. You shouldn't feel bad about Googling an answer.

If you have a modern smartphone that runs a recent version of Android, you also have access to another nice feature: voice recognition. Often you will have your hands full when working on an IT project. Instead of having to put down your task and then type a search into your smartphone, you simply say, "OK, Google," and then a phrase or question, such as, "how do I open a jammed CD drive?" Your Android phone should pick up on your voice and immediately respond with search results. Sometimes Google is so confident in the results that a computerized voice will actually read the answer to the question aloud. In any event, it sure beats having to drop everything to perform a Google search.

Oh, and one last thing—use Google. This isn't a paid advertisement; the natural language search and the quality of the search results are unmatched, in my opinion as both an IT person and a library professional. Google may slowly use these trillions of searches to build an artificial intelligence that will someday take over the world. But it is not today.

DAY-TO-DAY SUCCESS AND THE SPECTER OF PERFECTIONISM

The detailed nature of IT work lends itself to inherent perfectionism. It is easy to obsess over something as simple as the font on a screen saver, just because the look and presentation should be exactly right for the public machines. You must constantly run updates as well as do maintenance such as disk defragmentation.

A **font** is a particular visual style applied to text, which changes its appearance.
Defragmentation is a process whereby your computer places all of the data belonging to a particular file close together, which speeds up access to that file.

In my spare time (Ha!), my eyes must be open for the "next big thing" that will have an impact on technology in the library.

It's worth declaring up front—perfection is not possible with IT work, but some level of success is possible. The second you think you have it all nailed down, you don't. A component will fail, a new update will be pushed out, or driver software will become corrupt. Then you will start all over again, trying to shine Sisyphus's stone while it's rolling downhill. So go easy on yourself.

An **update** is a fix or correction to software, such as Microsoft Office, which is issued after the product is released.

Driver software is special software designed to instruct your computer how to interact with the components to which it is attached. For example, in order for a computer to communicate with an attached printer, the computer must have the correct driver software installed, which allows the computer to speak the language of the printer.

Figure out what your definition of perfection or success is. Is it applying updates within a week of being published? Is it 95 percent of the public computers up and running at any given time? Is it just treading water because you've been given a workload appropriate for three people? (This happens OFTEN.) Everyone's definition of success is a little bit different. Librarians are especially guilty of organizing things to near perfection. We pull a book from the shelf and relabel it if the Dewey Decimal call number is off by one one-thousandth from the correct heading. (For nonlibrarians, there really isn't much of a comparison here; it's like wrapping all of your Christmas gifts in coordinating colors, then taking out a spectrograph and analyzing those paper colors to make sure they really do match, and then taking the ones that don't and tearing off the paper and rewrapping them so that they do.)

IT work is not perfection. IT work is a constant climb to stay on top of updates and hardware issues, all the time keeping an eye on emerging trends so you can adopt new technology when the public and staff demand it. Add that to the fact that in small- or medium-sized libraries, you're often working with technology that should have been replaced years ago, but the budget doesn't allow it. It's twice as hard to maintain equipment that is obsolete. So if IT work in general is a climb, consider IT work in the public sector akin to a climb on a StairMaster. Most of the time, you're just treading in place.

That's not meant to suggest that you can't do really well as an IT person. It's just that the definition of success looks a little bit different for a one-person IT crew in a public library than it does for an IT department in a large corporation.

Success in the simplest sense could simply be defined as maintaining the status quo. Chances are, however, you are going to want to do more than that, especially if you've been assigned to fix some technology problems that may have been lingering for years before your arrival. Initial success will consist, then, of getting your IT system "back on its feet" and restoring as many things as possible to an operating condition. Once the initial triage is passed, your definition of success may revert to a status quo scenario in which an overall goal is to keep everything running. However, as previously mentioned, it is unlikely that you'll have a perfect record and will never have a machine that is out of service due to a hardware or software problem. So in that case, success is restoring the computer to service as soon as possible while still maintaining the other computers in service.

You may also define success by some of the other tasks that we have discussed in previous chapters. Success can take the form of meeting some or all of your long-term technology goals, or it can simply mean finding the money to replace an underperforming computer that is just too old to operate efficiently. Really, success is however you choose to define it, but it is important to make a concrete definition for success in your position.

Figure out what your definition of success is (it may be worth asking your supervisor for input as well) and then stick to it. Maybe even write it down and tack it to your wall. It's a reasonable goal that will help you put the work you are doing in perspective.

At the same time, when you meet your definition of success, or even approach it, you should be honest about it. Don't be modest about trumpeting your accomplishments to your superiors. Again, realize that your superior probably has very little or no experience with this type of work and doesn't understand that you're managing to control an essential service that is also one of the most dynamic—all by yourself. All the supervisor sees is the sign that says a computer is out of order, and the inevitable question that follows from him or her is, "Why?" Resist the temptation to be sarcastic—to say something along the lines of "Well, if you'd given me an assistant IT person, we wouldn't have those issues." First of all, that's a promise that you may not be able to keep. Even organizations with hundreds of IT employees occasionally have downtime. Second, it patronizes your supervisor. Instead, quickly and succinctly explain the situation with that particular machine and reassure them that it is on your work list to resolve. Then follow by explaining the success you have had, and point out that even though there is one computer out of order the majority of computers are up and running correctly most of the time. In fact, your success rate has been excellent since you're the only employee currently assigned to the task.

Even when everything is working perfectly, it is important to let your supervisor(s) know about your success. This is especially important on the performance evaluation, which is a permanent record that's kept of your successes. Fill either the verbal or written space on that evaluation with tales of how you've been able to do so much on your own.

Finally, don't be afraid to ask for a raise if you feel you deserve one. Many books and articles have been written on how to deal with your supervisor and on the best method to ask for more compensation. It's up to you to choose the method, but the message is clear: Don't sell yourself short. You are handling mission-critical services all by yourself and handling them well. You deserve to be rewarded for this work.

CHAPTER 3

Triage

Hopefully, the information technology (IT) responsibilities you've either been hired into or promoted into are consistent with what you were expecting when you agreed to take on these duties. If you didn't agree to anything but rather were pushed into the position, don't worry. Step by step, we are going to make this as painless as possible.

When you first enter an IT role, behave like a first responder. First responders have a checklist that they go through any time they are responding to an emergency call. Once they arrive, the item at the top of the checklist is: "Assess the situation/scene." In other words, observe what's going on, make a note of any critical issues that may be arising, and then based on that information, decide in which order you are going to treat the ailments. It does no good to arrive on the first day in this new position and run around trying to solve everybody's crises at once. You'll appear panicked, and that panic will quickly spread to other staff and perhaps even the public.

First Responder Checklist:

1. Assess the situation/scene
2. Look for clues that will help you isolate the problem
3. Get a history of the problem, if available
4. Listen to what others might tell you about the problem

Instead, take a moment to step back and assess everything. Try using the following method:

1. Find an empty bulletin board if one is available. If not, find a blank wall near your work area.
2. Obtain a notepad or scrap paper.
3. Cut or rip several strips of paper into approximately eight and half inches by two inches.
4. On each strip, write one technology issue that is currently occurring (i.e. "Printer not duplexing" or "Computer 6 is down").
5. Tape or pushpin these strips in a vertical series up and down the left edge of your bulletin board or wall.
6. Look at all the issues and determine which one is the highest priority. Unpin that issue and tack it to the right of the current top issue. This method will allow you to "leapfrog" one issue over another in priority.
7. When you have determined the order of the issues that need to be addressed, move all strips to the right until they are aligned one underneath another in a single vertical column.

Something as simple as outlining all of your issues so you can see them at once allows you to begin to understand what your top priorities are as you start work. If you have a more hands-on style supervisor, it would be worth asking what his or her priorities are as well. This will help you to get an understanding of the overall goals as you address technology issues.

You'll quickly find that some issues consistently slide to the bottom of the priority heap. This is a natural function of the method, which is also to determine that some things are not as much of a priority. These nonpriorities become your rainy-day projects. You may even find that over time you want to create two separate priority charts and keep your pool of low-priority items away from your pool of high-priority items.

If you've never done a prioritization scheme before, don't worry. Here are some suggestions on how to prioritize various issues, a sort of Maslow's Hierarchy of Needs for the IT world.

In order of highest priority, they are given as follows:

1. General building emergencies that affect IT. Examples: There's been a fire in the network room, you've taken a power surge and nothing is working, or there is no building power. You'll generally have help from your superiors in dealing with these types of issues and will hopefully be able to reclassify it quickly.
2. IT outages that affect the immediate operations of a library's primary customer services. Examples: You have no connection to the library's integrated library system (ILS) database, the circulation desk computers are not working, or patrons are unable to access the online public access catalog, aka the library catalog. The library website being down also goes into this category. More and more patrons use the library's website for their day-to-day library needs, and this makes it a mission-critical service.
3. Issues with backups. Backups, such as those done on a library server of the data on shared network drives, are also critical and should be functioning correctly at all times if possible. A priority 1 or 2 issue could occur at any moment, and if it does, you will need to have a backup available in the event data needs to be restored to new hardware (such as a new server).

4. IT outages that affect the immediate operations of other staff roles. Examples: The director's computer is not operating correctly. The Interlibrary Loan computer is not operating correctly. The program that allows cataloging of materials is not operating correctly. There is no shared access to network drives.
5. IT issues that affect public access to computers and other public technology. Presuming you don't have a larger network outage, individual public computers that are experiencing issues, along with related printers and other devices, should be classified here. Nobody wants to put up an "out of order" sign, but the world will not end if you do.
6. Windows updates, Java updates, Antivirus updates, etc. Failing to keep computers up-to-date on several critical programs can leave the computer vulnerable to a variety of security threats. It is important to make sure computers are up-to-date. Fortunately, since you generally set updates to run and then wait around while they do, you can use the free time to tackle priority 7.
7. IT issues that range from minor problems to irritations. Examples: The photocopier is leaving streaks on documents, staff members complain about programs popping up unexpectedly, staff would like to set their antivirus scans to run at a different time, etc.

Understand that with this list there are no hard-and-fast rules as to how you can prioritize things, unless your supervisor sets some priorities for you. Each individual situation is different, and if the director suddenly needs to make copies of a critical report, for example, the photocopier streaks may have to be fixed now and not later. Suddenly the photocopier's priority is raised in the hierarchy.

Once you have a list of your priorities, you can begin to tackle the most severe. With any luck, you won't have inherited an IT job while the library is in the middle of dealing with either a priority 1- or 2-type issue, though it DOES happen occasionally! Assuming you're at priority 3 or below for your most critical issue, you can start by determining if it is a network-level or individual hardware/software issue.

DETERMINING WHERE TO BEGIN

When diagnosing trouble with a computer, the first step is to determine if the issue is a phantom, which is simply a one-time problem. The easiest way to do this is to simply **power-cycle** the machine. To power-cycle a computer, shut it down normally if possible. Unplug the power cable from the back of the machine and then hold in the power button for ten seconds. You may see the power button light up momentarily as the last of the power is drained from the machine. Wait a whole minute, then plug in the machine again and power on the computer. If the computer comes back up as normal, the issue is resolved, and no action needs to be taken unless the issue recurs. You will be astonished at how often a power-cycle solves the problem. It should always be your first step unless you are positive it is a software configuration issue, such as, "I want to set up a screen saver because my computer doesn't have one." If you are trying to troubleshoot a problem, follow the earlier method to power-cycle rather than just click "Restart" from the Windows desktop. Power-cycling forces a cold boot because you are completely powering off the machine, draining any remaining power, letting it sit, and then repowering the machine. A warm boot simply repeats the start-up sequence without physically removing power to the device.

A **cold boot** means that power is completely removed from a computer, then power restored and the machine turned on.

A **warm boot** is more commonly known as a **restart** or reboot.

Even though we don't think of computers as having moving parts, they do need time to sit cold, for a couple of reasons. First, there are actually several moving parts inside computers, not the least of which are the quickly rotating platters that make up your typical hard disk drive. If you've never seen a cutaway view of a hard drive in action, I encourage you to search for a video online. It's more like your father's record player than anyone, least of all IT professionals, would care to admit. However, even nonmoving parts benefit from a cold boot. A cold boot ensures that RAM, short for random access memory, has a chance to be completely cleared. It also makes sure that the processor and its cache (built-in memory) has time to clear to a zero state. During a cold boot, all activity inside the computer completely stops and then starts again. You can be assured that the computer really is restarting with a clean slate.

Random Access Memory (RAM) is temporary memory that is erased whenever power is turned off.

A **memory leak** is when a program fails to free memory that is not being used.

Phantom issues with computers are actually very common. One typical example is a memory leak. When software such as Microsoft Word is loaded into RAM, it uses the space in RAM to store information as necessary until it is ready to be processed. Part of good programming is that the software should use no more RAM than is necessary and should free the RAM when it is no longer in use by the program. A memory leak is caused because the Windows operating system protects memory space reserved for the program until the software releases it. Any memory a program reserves takes away from the grand total that is left for other programs to use. If the program fails to release the memory, it simply remains unavailable indefinitely. If a memory leak such as this is severe, it can impair a program's ability to function. No program clears perfectly out of memory, but usually the memory leaks are extremely small. Over time, however, these leaks can build up and begin to cause problems. This is one of the reasons (though certainly not the only reason) that your organization may already have in place a standard schedule for rebooting machines that are on all of the time, such as servers.

If the problem comes back when you reboot the computer, it's time to dig just a little bit deeper. First, is this problem occurring on only one machine? Several? All of them? If every machine in the building is having the same issue, you can suspect a network-level issue. Some indicators that point to network-level issues are as follows:

1. You cannot access the Internet on any machine or can do so on very few machines.
2. You cannot log into the computer, and you have a domain setup with active directory, such as when you log into a server and share network drives.

3. You cannot connect to network services or the Internet and the Windows operating system complains about having "limited or no network connection." Usually, this shows next to the clock in the system tray of the Windows desktop.
4. You cannot access the Internet and the Windows operating system complains about having no access to the Internet. This may appear in various dialogs or in the system tray.
5. You cannot access other internal network services such as networked printers.

Within buildings, such as your library building, networks are connected using a standard called **Ethernet**. In years past, Ethernet had competitors such as Token Ring, which was another standard that set the network up in a different fashion than that of Ethernet. In the modern network, however, Ethernet is the only widely used standard. For you as a library IT technician, this means that physically all of the Ethernet network plugs and cabling will be interchangeable and network equipment (discussed in later chapters) will behave in the manner that you expect and transmit data like you expect, no matter which vendor is responsible for producing it.

A **standard** means a declared manner in which all networks of this type must operate so that cables, equipment, and data transmission schemes are compatible with one another across all vendors.

On your desktop computer, the Ethernet port is normally located on the back of the case. Depending on the computer, it could be located anywhere from the top to the bottom of the case, but will be grouped with other ports on the back of the machine. An Ethernet port looks like a telephone port, but the plug (male connector) is wider than a telephone plug so that the two cannot be mixed up. Ethernet plugs simply snap into ports and are released by squeezing a small tab on the underside of the plug (again exactly like a traditional wired telephone plug).

A **port** is a female connector located on a piece of equipment. It accepts the male connectors from a particular type of cable.
Link lights are lights on a port which indicate that the cable is correctly connected to equipment on both ends of the cable.

One handy starting point for diagnosing network issues are the link lights located at the top of the Ethernet port on the back of each machine. There are generally either one or two link lights on an Ethernet port, and they are normally either green or yellow. The lights are too small to see unless they are lit; when lit, they give the appearance that the bottom two corners of the Ethernet port are lit up. Link lights serve two purposes. First, they confirm that you are connected to networking equipment somewhere. This is very handy because networking rooms are often far away from the computers they serve.

Second, they confirm that data is flowing between the computer and the network equipment. Some link lights also serve a third purpose—to confirm the speed at which the equipment is connected (10 Mbps, 100 Mbps, or 1,000 Mbps). Absence of any link lights on a Windows-based computer could indicate a variety of issues. Common issues might include the following:

1. The network cable is disconnected on one end or the other.
2. The network interface is disabled in the Windows operating system.
3. Incorrect drivers are loaded for the Ethernet chip or card in the computer.
4. The networking equipment on the other end of the cable needs to be rebooted or has ceased to function.
5. The Ethernet chip or card in the computer has been shut off through the computer's BIOS/CMOS setup screen.
6. The network card or chip in the computer has ceased to function.
7. The network cable is physically broken.

The network interface getting disabled in Windows is actually fairly common. When any software is granted administrator rights (the little box in Windows 7 that dims the screen, pops up, and says, "Do You Wish to Continue?"), one of the rights the software has is the ability to enable or disable a network interface. If the interface is disabled, no link lights will appear.

Network cables are also commonly disconnected. Especially in older machines, the Ethernet ports tend to become loose over time, and you may find that if you wiggle a plug enough a short occurs and the network connection is dropped. Depending on the situation, you may have to replace the cable or the network interface.

A **motherboard** is the heart of the computer, containing the processor and other core circuits that are necessary for the computer to function.

Modern onboard network interfaces (those where the Ethernet jack is attached directly to a chip on the motherboard) are also notorious for giving up the ghost. Most of the computer components in your average machine are mass produced in various foreign factories. The complete machine is assembled state-side (sometimes not even that), and then the machine is tested and shipped to you.

Even if the issue is not readily apparent during quality control testing at the factory, a component with a manufacturing issue is a time bomb for your computer. Any bit of data could be the one that causes the network interface to stop working. On top of this, if your building experiences a power surge, Ethernet interfaces on computers seem to be the number one damaged and failed component. I don't know why this is—perhaps because the network equipment provides an alternate path to ground. Your mileage may vary, but you should know that they do fail from time to time.

It is unlikely but not impossible that the network equipment on the other end of the cable could be responsible for your problem. Modern network equipment is designed to be relatively tough. Mid-range to high-end equipment also has the ability to reboot itself and perform other corrections when errors occur. However, networking equipment has a processor like other computer equipment, and as such, it could conceivably lock up and need to be rebooted from time to time. However, if you find that you are rebooting a specific piece of network equipment more often than about once every six months, you should look into other causes, get the issue diagnosed by another professional, or replace the faulty equipment.

If you determine that the network issue is at the computer level, you can proceed to correct the issue by searching Google for the type of problem that you are experiencing. This may require you to open the computer to retrieve the model number of the Ethernet chip, which is printed directly on the chip. You can identify the Ethernet chip as generally the one closest to the network jack that protrudes from the rear of the computer.

Chips

Chips, as opposed to other board components, are the black or gray squares with numbers and writing on them. By the way, the combination of all chips on a board and how they work in tandem has come to be known as a **chipset**. Once in a while, you will read references about updating the chipset driver.

Chips, more formally called integrated circuits, are groups of miniaturized electronic components, packaged together, which perform specific tasks in support of the larger computer system as a whole.

If the network issue is not at the individual computer, you've determined that you have a larger networking issue affecting a variety of different computers. Proceed to this book's chapter on networking to determine your next steps in diagnosis. If you have not read that whole chapter, be sure to read it from the beginning, as it is important to have a basic idea of how the network is laid out before starting to troubleshoot why network services are unavailable.

CHAPTER 4

Troubleshooting the Individual Computer

If you've determined that the issue you are trying to diagnose is not related to the network, you can safely assume that the issue has to do with the individual hardware or software of the computer. This section will walk you through the boot process of a computer, stopping to explain the major points at which failure could occur.

You may or may not have had the opportunity to put your hands into a computer case up until this point. Let's begin by looking at the desktop computer. The traditional desktop computer is a beige or black, rather nondescript-looking metal box that sits on your floor or desktop. You plug the box into wall power, plug your components into the box (monitor, mouse, keyboard, etc.), press the power button, and away it goes.

It's helpful, at this point, to get a brief overview of what's happening on the inside of a computer. Traditionally, a computer has one main board, called the **motherboard.** The central processing unit (CPU) plugs into this board in a special socket designed for it (Figure 4.1). **Expansion cards,** which are smaller boards that plug into the main board at a 90-degree angle, allow the computer to provide major functions such as video output, sound output, faxing, and networking (Figure 4.2).

At one time, the only service integrated directly into the motherboard was the keyboard interface. Today, many components that once required separate cards are integrated into the motherboard. (As a historical note, if you call these cards "daughter boards," that's really, really dating you.) Services such as video output, Ethernet or network interface, mouse recognition, and sound output are all permanently attached to the motherboard on specialized chips. Each service has at least one chip—a chip for video output, a chip for

Figure 4.1 A motherboard with CPU socket

Figure 4.2 An expansion card

Figure 4.3   The inside of a desktop computer

Ethernet, a chip for USB recognition (such as mice and keyboards), and a chip for sound, as well as a chip for hard drive control, etc. This is a blessing, as it takes up much less room in the case, and you are less prone to physical issues such as a card coming loose or gathering too much dust and shorting. On the other hand, everything being built into one board increases the likelihood that you may have to replace the motherboard (i.e., the whole computer) to fix a broken component, if there is no room for an expansion card to restore the service.

All told, an actual desktop computer looks like the one in Figure 4.3.

When you need to put your hands into a computer case, follow these steps.

Step One: Release the case. Some desktop cases are now "quick release" and have one side that slides off quite easily if you know where the release is located. The location of the latch varies by manufacturer. For example, one popular manufacturer places a latch on the rear of the case at the top. Pulling this latch toward the rear of the case causes one of the side panels to pop free. Many other desktops have two large thumbscrews on the rear of the case, which secure one side. Removing the two thumbscrews allows the side to slide free.

Thumbscrews are like regular case screws, but with exceptionally oversized screw heads. The large size of the screw head allows the screws to generally be operated using only one's thumbs.

Step Two: Once inside, make sure the computer is unplugged,
Step Three: Drain any remaining power by holding down the power button on the front of the computer case for ten seconds.

Desktop computers are usually manufactured such that the case is divided up into four distinct quadrants, each having a different purpose. In Figure 4.3, A is the top of the case, B is the bottom of the case, C is the front of the case, and D is the back of the case.

The computer's power supply (E) is responsible for converting the power coming out of your wall (which would blow up a computer many times over) and "stepping it down" into voltages that the computer can work with. The excess power is mostly converted into heat, which is vented out the rear of the case. Some power supplies have their own fan, and some do not. The power supply provides constant power to the motherboard so that a simple touch of a button on the front case of the computer can start the boot process. Suspect a bad power supply if you plug the computer into a known good outlet, but the computer does not power on when you press the front button.

The drive "bays" (F) are for larger types of drives, such as the DVD-RW drive. The drive is mounted with either screws or quick-release tabs to the sides of the bay. The front of the drive is finished with a trim piece called a **bezel** and sticks out the front of the case to allow the user access even when the case is closed. Two separate cables connect the drive to both the motherboard and the power supply. Fortunately, it is impossible to mix up these two cables; they won't fit on the wrong connectors.

A typical computer case can hold between one and four hard disk drives. Most off-the-shelf desktop computers only come with one hard drive. These drives are mounted to the bays (G) that hold them with either screws or quick-release tabs. Again, each drive connects to both the motherboard and the power supply with two cables that cannot be mixed up.

Finally, we have the motherboard itself (H). The CPU is located underneath the fan. Memory (RAM) goes in the slots just to the left of the CPU (I), and expansion cards, if there are any, go in the row of connectors near the back of the case (so the business-end of the cards can stick out of slots in the rear of the case). You may also have another case fan mounted to the rear of the computer. This fan connects to the motherboard (not the power supply) so that the computer can vary the speed of the fan as necessary and also turn it on and off if, for example, the computer is put into sleep mode.

A desktop computer is actually a variety of integrated services and components tied together into a complete functioning unit. Now that we know how a desktop computer is put together, we can make a quick-and-dirty extrapolation about other common types of computers. Fortunately, it is unlikely that you will ever be called upon to repair anything except a desktop computer. Repairing other types of computers, such as those mentioned later, is best left to a specialist.

A laptop is simply a desktop computer with everything, including the screen, integrated into a single portable unit. All components of a laptop are reduced in size considerably by using advanced manufacturing techniques. A battery is added under the motherboard to power the laptop when it is away from a wall power source. Hard drive and memory are both located underneath the motherboard as well. When you lay a keyboard on top of this sandwich (with an integrated trackpad) and then top it off with an LCD, plasma, or LED monitor and give everything a custom case, you have a laptop.

To build a tablet, we reduce the size of the motherboard even further. Data storage is probably entirely solid state. Think of storage on a flash drive or SD card as opposed to a traditional hard drive.

A **flash drive**, also called a thumb drive, is a small, rectangular storage device that plugs into your USB port. It functions in the same way as a traditional disk drive; files can be saved to and opened directly from a flash drive.

A **SD card** is a flat, nearly square chip that slides into a compatible SD card slot on your computer. It is a storage device, so files can be written to and read from a SD card in the same way as a flash drive. SD cards were made popular by digital cameras, which required a very small form of storage due to the limited size of the camera. Today, the standard has an even smaller physical size, known as a micro-SD card.

Extra storage is obtained by inserting a very small removable SD card into the outside of the case. The touch screen is placed directly on top of the motherboard, and some larger, non-essential ports are removed. Finally a specialized, non-removable battery is added. Each model of tablet has a customized case because it has to fit so closely with the footprint of the various internal components. The ridiculously tight fit of these devices is why it is ill advised to take apart your iPhone or other mobile or tablet device (even though there is no shortage of businesses on the Internet willing to sell you a case "cracking" kit).

Finally, to build a smartphone, the smallest of the small, all ports except mini or micro USB and headphone are removed (Figure 4.4). Some phones also have a well-hidden port for an external micro-SD card for extra storage space. A smartphone is effectively a small tablet, with the addition of cellular phone components that allow the device to communicate with your carrier's network. The other addition is a small card like a mini SD card called a Single In-line Memory Module (SIMM). The SIMM card provides the phone with vendor-specific information. If you keep your phone but change networks, the SIMM card is what will be replaced by the new carrier. This is much more common in Europe, where virtually all phones are purchased at the retail store (or ordered online) like any other computing device and then taken to your carrier of choice for a SIMM card. In Europe, phones will work no matter which carrier you use or if you switch carriers.

The general trend is to make devices ever smaller, although we have definitely hit the point where devices can be manufactured too small to be practical. Phones and tablets serve different roles, but the 10-inch iPad coexists happily alongside the iPhone. Both benefit from the fact that there is a common interface between them. The same can be said for Android tablets and phones. If you like to trend-spot, there are several Android-based watches coming on to the market, which run an even more simplified version of apps and are the physical manifestation of Dick Tracy's watch from years ago. They may have uses, but size will be a limiting factor.

Figure 4.4 A smartphone (left) and tablet computer

TROUBLESHOOT THE BOOT

Now you know that there are many individual components that can fail or malfunction inside a machine. People tend to think of computers as a "unit," which either works or doesn't. But it's really more like a car, minus the fan belts (although it does have at least one fan until you get down to tablet size). Many components make up the whole, and most times it is worth it to diagnose the problem rather than just throw out the unit and buy a new one.

Let's follow a computer through the start-up process and examine where things might go wrong.

Booting is actually a shortened version of another word, "bootstrapping." This is the process by which a computer literally "pulls itself up by its bootstraps" from a dead piece of silicon and metal. The computer comes to life, progressively loading instructions and software such that, within a minute or two, the system presents itself through a monitor as the Windows desktop that we have come to know.

The process of booting begins when the motherboard receives a signal that the computer should power on. Long ago, the motherboard was completely dead until a rocker-switch was snapped "ON." Then power was applied to the power supply unit, which in turn provided the power that the motherboard needed to operate. Nowadays, the motherboard is continuously powered by the power supply unit but is in an "OFF" state until a digital signal (a button press) is received from the button on the front of the machine.

When the motherboard goes to an "ON" state, the processor immediately requests instructions from the **Basic Input/Output System (BIOS)**. The BIOS is a chip located on the motherboard, which controls the very first moments of a computer's boot cycle. The first set of instructions in BIOS is simply where to find the next set of instructions in the BIOS and **Complementary Metal Oxide Semiconductor (CMOS)**. CMOS stores some basic settings for how the computer should behave (including some that you are able to modify). The BIOS itself is permanent and cannot normally be modified, so the CMOS stores settings instead. If you've ever seen a message like "Press F2 to enter setup" when you start your computer, pressing F2 will drop you into the CMOS setup screen. People often state that this is the BIOS setup screen, but that is not entirely correct; BIOS dictates what the menus say, but the changes are saved to the CMOS.

BIOS performs some low-level checks on the functioning of computer hardware before the boot process continues. These tests are known collectively as the **Power on Self Test (POST)**. Memory is verified and tested, expansion cards (if any) are tested, various chip components such as Ethernet and video are tested, and finally drives, such as the hard disk drive, are detected. Once the primary drive is detected, the BIOS can go to that drive's **boot sector** to find the location of the next instructions to load from the drive. Note that most machines have a "Quick Boot" setting that allows you to skip some more expansive tests in the POST. This saves time but also may limit the diagnostic ability of POST. If you are experiencing trouble, try disabling the quick boot option and see if expanded tests give you any more information about the problem.

The method to disable quick boot varies by manufacturer, but here are some general directions:

- Enter the CMOS setup screen by pressing F2 or another appropriate key immediately after start-up, when prompted by the computer.
- Look for an option labeled "Quick Boot."
- Following the directions provided along the side or bottom of the screen, change the value of "Quick Boot" from enabled to disabled.
- Press Esc to exit set-up, confirming that you want to save the changes.
- The computer will reboot and perform all of the normal tests, including those skipped by Quick Boot.

Computer errors are generally divided into two types: fatal and non-fatal. Non-fatal errors are those that allow the computer to recover and continue, either automatically or after the computer user confirms that they have addressed the error (e.g., by clicking "OK" in a dialog box). Fatal errors, on the other hand, are errors that stop the computer in its tracks. In these instances, the computer must be rebooted, as the normal sequence of events for the computer cannot continue. For example, if the computer cannot detect any drive at all to boot from (such as a hard drive) it may report this with a fatal error action, meaning you will have to correct the issue and then reboot the computer to try again.

The BIOS POST is the first place that problems might crop up with a boot cycle. If possible, the BIOS will display an error message if one exists and halt the boot until the issue is resolved. A common error is some form of "No Keyboard Detected—Press F1 to continue." For what it's worth, the "Press F1 to continue" text is automatically appended to non-fatal BIOS errors; the computer really has no understanding that you can't press F1 on a keyboard that wasn't detected.

You may also hear a series of beeps coming from the machine, especially if there is nothing displayed on the computer screen. Listen for how many beeps are there, if they are long or short, high or low, and if they repeat or do not repeat. The beeps are the computer communicating to you that something has gone terribly wrong. The sounds a computer makes become especially important if the error (such as a memory or video error) prevents the computer from displaying an error message at all. **Beep codes** are quite accurate at conveying information about problems. For example, if there is a memory issue, the computer has a specific type of beep code that will tell you so. Google's search results will help you diagnose the problem.

The search strategy for locating beep codes online is fairly straightforward. You need to search a manufacturer name and the phrase "BIOS beep codes." The best possible method is to search the actual manufacturer of the BIOS, such as "American Megatrends." The manufacturer of the BIOS can be found along the top or bottom of the CMOS setup screens. If you cannot enter the CMOS setup for some reason, search instead for the make and model of the computer in place of the manufacturer in your search string.

The most common issue that prevents display of an error message, besides a memory error, is a video card or chip error. If you have a video card installed, it may have come loose or failed. Try switching video cards if you have a spare. If the video is controlled by a chip on the motherboard, you may have to locate a different video card to use instead (again with the cheap, failed motherboard components).

Presuming you are able to get at least a rudimentary video display out of the computer, a BIOS/CMOS-based message should tell you what the problem is if there is one. Most errors are self-explanatory (i.e., "Keyboard not detected"), but a few are cryptic. Look them up using Google to determine an exact cause or resolution. Keep in mind that very little of the BIOS instructions have to do with higher-order software, so if the computer stops at this point you are virtually always dealing with a hardware issue of some sort.

BUT, BUT . . . UEFI!

If you have a computer that was purchased recently, you may have heard quite a bit about **Unified Extensible Firmware Interface (UEFI)**. This is one of those topics that, again, people tend to make way more complicated than it needs to be. What you need to know is this: UEFI is a successor to BIOS. Computer advancement has brought us many good things, but BIOS is quite literally the same technology that we had when Windows 3.1

was king in the early 1990s. Computer processors have recently undergone what is known as an "architecture change" from 32-bit to 64-bit. As always, this allows the computer to do more and faster, but programs that run on the processor have to be written specifically to run on it. Traditional BIOS does not really support 64-bit architecture (or rather, 64-bit architecture does not support the ancient BIOS technology). Therefore, a successor was needed to BIOS. Cue UEFI.

If you've taken a look at a traditional BIOS setup screen, you already know that the interface and options leave much to be desired. UEFI solves this problem, among many others, by reimagining the way a computer boots. Rather than a clunky, limited setup screen pulled from a dedicated chip on the computer, UEFI is, effectively, a miniature graphical operating system that allows you to immediately control many more settings of your computer, launch start-up repair, and activate a host of other functions, all *before* you boot the primary operating system. So while UEFI replaces traditional BIOS in the boot sequence and provides all the control functionality of traditional BIOS, it is a much, much more versatile system and provides many more features than a traditional BIOS.

Again, if you're just gaining experience with the menus you can access prior to booting an operating system, UEFI won't throw you off at all. However, if you have had some experience with the setup screens of traditional BIOS (Figure 4.5), you may be

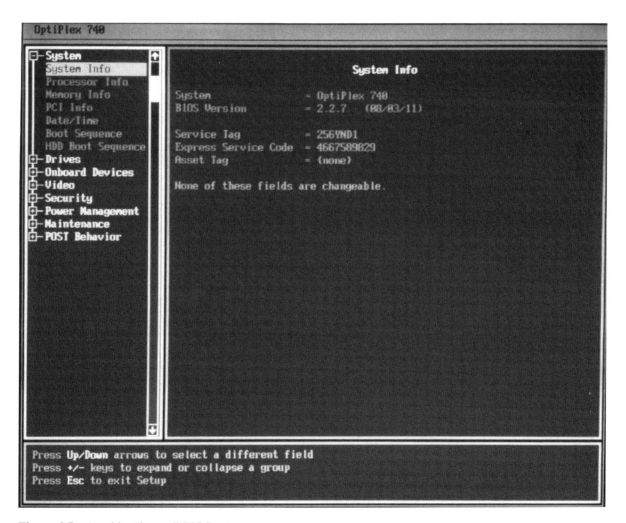

Figure 4.5   An older "legacy" BIOS setup screen

momentarily disoriented by UEFI. You'll quickly find the similarities, however, along with some nice new features, such as navigation that supports point-and-click selection and scrolling.

One more note: **BIOS**, again, stands for **Basic Input Output System**. We're used to referring to the chip with the clunky 1990s' menus as the BIOS, but really UEFI can be considered a BIOS as well, and you'll sometimes hear it referred to as UEFI BIOS. But don't be confused. Though it controls some of the same features, it is a totally different technology from the old traditional BIOS chip. When the rest of this chapter refers to BIOS, it can refer to either traditional BIOS or UEFI. The text was written such that they are interchangeable unless noted.

BACK TO THE START-UP SEQUENCE

Once the BIOS POST is complete, the computer will either beep once or not at all, and the Windows logo (or a nondescript scroll bar in Windows Vista) should appear as the operating system begins to load. Operating systems are the primary piece of software that allows you to interact with your computer. Without an operating system loaded, the computer is not in a usable state. Some operating systems are text based, such as MS-DOS and UNIX. However, this type of operating system has been largely overtaken in desktop environments by operating systems with a **graphical user interface (GUI)**. As the name suggests, GUI operating systems such as Microsoft Windows allow users to interact with the computer using graphics. It's now so common to double-click on icons and use the desktop that we rarely stop to think that it wasn't always that way. For the purposes of this book, we will be using Microsoft Windows as our base operating system. The version isn't important; again, this book will explain how to diagnose a variety of different scenarios in general terms. Learning how to access a particular feature in your version of the control panel, however, can be accomplished with a quick Google search.

At this point, behind the scenes, Windows is loading its own components, which include operating system files as well as drivers. Drivers are software that helps Windows know how to interact with a specific piece of hardware, such as your network card. If all of these components load, then Windows moves forward with allowing you to interact with the computer on your own. However, if one of these components fails to load, Windows may either suddenly reboot, it may display a cryptic blue screen, or it may just freeze while displaying the Windows logo. One of the reasons the start-up screen is animated (other than to look pretty) is to indicate to you that Windows is actually still loading files. If the animation freezes, you can begin to be concerned that something has gone terribly wrong.

On earlier versions of Windows, it was more common for Windows component files to become corrupt. Cryptic messages such as "NTLDR is missing" would appear, forcing you to search (sometimes in vain) for a way to repair your installation of Windows. Fortunately, in my experience, these issues have become less common with Windows 7 and Windows 8. Much more common are driver issues, where an incorrect driver is loaded for a device, such as your network card. When Windows tries to communicate with that device using the driver, the device either doesn't respond or sends back garbage that Windows can't understand. Either of these problems can cause what's known as a **kernel panic** (no kidding, that's the name!).

In this scenario, the core routines of the Windows operating system don't know how to handle the error, which kills the operating system program altogether (a fatal error).

As a result, the computer either triggers an automatic reboot and tries again or throws up a "blue screen of death" and stops cold. Most anybody who has used Windows for any length of time is familiar with the so-called **blue screen of death**, which earned that moniker because it is a rather alarming shade of blue and is the last screen displayed before the Windows operating system gives up for good and terminates its own program. The screen contains a number that identifies the crash and also usually names the specific type of crash (such as IRQL_NOT_LESS_OR_EQUAL) and identifies the offending file that caused the crash, if there was one. The crash number, type of crash, and file that caused the crash (if any) can help you determine why the crash occurred. Chances are, if you run it through Google, you'll find that there are bunches of other people who have had the same problem with the same file, and some suggested resolutions for the issue.

On some flavors of Windows 7 and 8, the default action is to cue a blue screen of death followed immediately by an automatic reboot. This process happens so fast that most times you don't see the blue screen at all. This completely defeats the purpose of a kernel panic, which is to dump the crash information you need to the screen so that the issue won't occur again. Instead, the net effect on newer computers is that they appear to be stuck in an endless reboot cycle, when really there is something else entirely going on behind the scenes. Your computer may also automatically offer you the option to enter **safe mode** after the reboot (Figure 4.6).

Safe Mode

Safe mode is a Windows utility that allows you to gain control of Windows to determine what is wrong and fix it. When you enter safe mode, Windows loads a minimal amount of components and very basic, common drivers instead of using its normal components

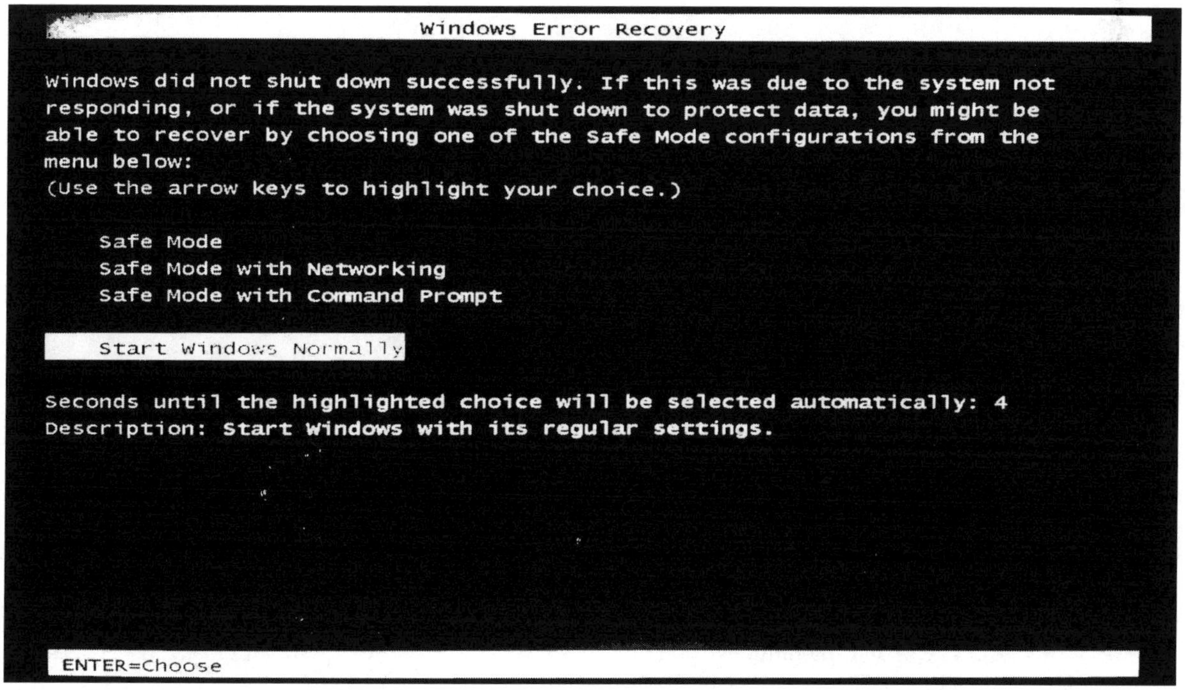

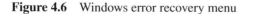

Figure 4.6 Windows error recovery menu

and drivers to load. This often allows the computer to complete the boot sequence and enter Windows. Some services, such as wireless networking, may be unavailable (the drivers aren't loaded), and you may find that your screen is set to a very low resolution because a basic video driver is being used. Despite this, however, Windows does allow you to control your computer and make changes to it using the Windows interface, which means you can often load the correct software or fix whatever else may be offending the computer.

How to use safe mode to fix problems:

1. Reboot the computer.
2. When the manufacturer's logo appears (before the Windows logo appears), begin pressing the F8 key about once per second.
3. Select either "Safe Mode" or "Safe Mode with networking" from the menu that appears, depending on whether you think you will need to download from the Internet during the session.
4. If step 2 does not get you to the safe mode selection menu, Google instructions for entering safe mode for your version of Windows.
5. Once Windows safe mode has launched, search the **error logs** for a problem.

Windows safe mode is actually quite simple to activate and use. How to examine the logs to find a problem is discussed later.

Logs are automatic records kept by the computer of various events that occur in the operating system. Error logs, for example, are records kept by the operating system about various problems encountered. Each time an error occurs, the operating system automatically "logs" it to a file, which includes the type and severity of the error and the date and time that it occurred. Users can review these log files to determine when certain events occurred within the system, which helps track down problems.

USING THE EVENT VIEWER

It's fortunate that even though Windows sometimes runs into trouble, it does an admirable job of logging any problems for later review by an administrator. To review these logs, you will use a program called **Event Viewer**.

To use Event Viewer, follow the steps:

1. Press ⊞ + R to open the Run dialog box.
2. Type "eventvwr.msc" and press Enter.
3. In the left pane, select "System," "Applications," or "Security" to view the log entries for that particular category.
4. Sort the log entries by time or severity and look for a log entry that occurred around the time of your last crash.
5. The offending entry will be classified as an error, not as a warning or information.
6. Right-click on the suspected problem entry and click "Properties" to view details of the error.

7. The Properties of the item will list all of the details that would have been available on the blue screen of death.
8. Look for a common name for the error, such as "IRQL_NOT_LESS_OR_EQUAL," and an offending filename, such as "xyz.sys."
9. Input this information into Google to find causes and solutions for the error.

Once you have a solution to your problem, chances are you will have to implement that solution while you are still in safe mode. Once the fix is implemented (such as installing a new driver), simply reboot to return to normal Windows mode.

By understanding the boot cycle of a computer and where to check for error logging, you can effectively determine issues that may be preventing your computer from booting. Because computers are so complex, there are a variety of features built into the computer and into Windows itself that aid in the diagnosis of malfunctions and errors. Understanding how to access and use these utilities will hopefully allow you to diagnose and correct what would otherwise be unrecoverable errors.

CHAPTER 5

Mobile Devices

We've come a long way in the past 20 years. Beginning in 1987, the popular television show *Star Trek: The Next Generation* featured several characters, including Captain Jean Luc Picard, not only using touch screen computers but also carrying around school-slate-sized devices (implied to be computers) that were 100 percent operated by touch. At the time, such devices were pure fiction.

Today we have an ever-expanding wireless data network, consisting of both Wi-Fi "hot spots" and cell tower data. We have an array of mobile devices such as smartphones, smart watches, tablets, eReaders, digital cameras, and more that operate on long-lasting rechargeable batteries and are completely touch-operated; no keyboard or other input device is necessary. They come in a variety of sizes and shapes, from the pocket "smartphone" to the very same slate-sized tablet device that was hypothesized so many years ago. Smart watches are also becoming available at time of this writing, which are a size smaller than even the smartphone.

A whole industry has sprung up around supporting these devices that are independent from the larger desktop and laptop brethren. Rather than Microsoft being the dominant player in the mobile device category, Apple computer and Android both hold major segments of the operating system market. Companies that traditionally have done well with desktops and laptops such as Dell computer have little or no inroads into the miniature mobile world, where players such as Motorola ("Moto" smartphones) and Samsung ("S" series of phones and tablets) are major influences. Apple computer is one of the few companies that has managed a complete crossover between the two worlds, and it is worth noting that Apple is not considered to be "IBM compatible," which is the traditional name for all other laptops and desktops on the market that aren't Apple architecture. The larger point being made here is that mobile devices such as laptops, smartphones, eReaders, tablets, and tablet computers such as the Microsoft Surface Pro aren't simply an "extension" of traditional desktop computers. It's not as if "I'm replacing my desktop computers, and Dell tells me the next generation of my model of desktop is actually a mobile device." No, on the contrary, mobile devices are an entirely *separate* segment of technology that exists independently from traditional desktops. This will greatly affect how your library treats such devices.

WIRELESS INTERNET

It is no secret that many millions of Americans own at least one mobile device. As a result of this, at the very least, it is imperative that your library provide free wireless Internet access, if at all possible. Because of the ever-increasing use of mobile devices, the expectation has become that many public spaces will provide wireless Internet access. If you want patrons to continue coming to the library for traditional activities such as work and study, you will have to come to terms with the idea that work and study is now done via computer. And because your patrons aren't going to haul a desktop computer back and forth from their house to the library, if they bring their own personal machine (which they are very likely to do), it *will* be a mobile device, and the expectation will be that their local public library *will* provide wireless Internet access.

If you feel that your current Internet speeds cannot successfully support a wireless access point or wireless router, it may be time to look at upgrading your Internet connection speed. This depends greatly upon the load (number of users) that you expect to utilize the connection at any one time. As a general guideline, as of this writing, a speed that is 5 Mbps or less can be considered too slow for practical use by the public.

First, you will need to find out who your current Internet service provider is. Give them a call and ask them what kind of a deal they are offering on an Internet service speed upgrade. You might be surprised. Always start by asking your current Internet service provider, as it is generally simpler and requires less downtime for your current ISP to increase your speed rather than a new ISP to completely replace your current company. If your current ISP does not have the offerings you are looking for, you may want to broaden your search to other local companies, including the local telephone company and the local cable company. Remember that depending upon the rules of your organization and the laws of your city and state, you may be required to either obtain a certain number of comparable quotes to show due diligence in investigating for budget purposes or you may be required to go through a formal bidding process, in which each vendor provides you with their best deal based on your requirements and then your organization selects the bid that is the best fit and most cost-effective. See Chapter 12, "Procurement," for more details on how to begin a request for bids or request for proposals process.

Wireless Internet access is now arguably a "core service" of the public library since so many of the non-book tasks that patrons do in a library now involve some type of mobile device.

A **wireless router** is a device that can create and sustain a wireless network without any additional equipment. A link to the Internet is plugged into the router, and the router manages the process of sending appropriate traffic to and from connected wireless devices.

A **wireless access point** is simply a wireless doorway into your existing network. It allows wireless devices to join your existing wired network in the same way that wired computers do. A wireless access point lacks the ability to route data and as such it can only be connected to an existing wired network, as it relies on a router elsewhere in the network to manage the flow of data.

Your wireless Internet setup does not have to be exceptionally complicated. In a small library, one wireless Internet transmitter (either a wireless router or wireless access point) may be all that you need to provide adequate coverage throughout the building. It is important to cover as much of the building as physically possible; don't rely on signage that says "wireless Internet area" to direct patrons to where they can receive a signal. Patrons are going to sit where they want regardless of the signage, and if the wireless Internet does not work, then they are going to leave, not reorient themselves according to some virtual boundary. Chapters 10 and 11 on networking in this book provide additional information and tips on wireless routers and wireless access points. Read and study those; it will help you determine the theory of wireless transmitters in your building. Basically, the rules for putting up a wireless transmitter are the same rules you'd use to fly a helicopter. First, put it up high, and second, avoid obstructions between mobile devices such as laptops and the transmitter. These might include walls, columns, and other building features. Also, avoid putting the transmitter near anything that puts off a large amount of electromagnetic interference, such as fluorescent light fixtures, microwaves, or cordless phones. Placing a wireless transmitter on the ceiling is ideal, if it is feasible. Also, if the wireless signal must go through walls, consider an additional transmitter on the other side in order to ensure that the signal is well received.

LOANING MOBILE DEVICES

Though your library may support mobile devices through the use of wireless access points or wireless routers, there is another facet to mobile device access. Working in rural libraries you will notice, as other librarians have, that many of the patrons we serve do not have access to mobile devices, even though the patrons could probably benefit from such access. That raises an important question: Are "loanable" mobile devices a service that the small library should provide? In other words, should the library, using taxpayer funds, purchase mobile devices of some type that are loanable to patrons? Such a program raises a whole host of questions and often creates more problems than it solves.

Having managed a laptop checkout program in two separate libraries, my advice is this: Only start such a program if you are prepared for the extra work it will entail and only if you are sure you are prepared to replace devices that may be damaged or destroyed. Once you start a program like this, the patrons come to expect the service, and it is very hard to stop. It is not only additional equipment that you have to replace if it wears out or breaks, but it is also additional equipment that you now have to work into your upgrade cycle and your very limited technology budget.

If you do decide to loan mobile devices, the first question is: What type of device are you going to loan? Smartphones are probably out because you don't want library patrons calling Timbuktu on library equipment. So this leaves you with laptops and tablets. For the sake of argument, we are going to lump eReaders such as the Kindle Fire and Nook with the rest of the tablet category. The functions they perform are only important when it comes to what your patrons demand. If patrons don't care about apps but only want to use digital books, then eReaders will work fine and it isn't necessary to get full-featured tablets. However, if patrons demand fully functional devices, you'll probably have to look past the eReaders to a full tablet.

Second, are the devices going to be used in the library only, or are patrons allowed to take the devices home? And another question to make things more complicated: if patrons take the devices home, how are you going to protect them in transit? Considering the condition of some of the books that libraries get back from patrons, it is imperative that you have some kind of carrying case in which patrons can transport the device if it is going to leave the building.

Next, consider how you are going to care for the device from patron to patron. In Chapter 11, "Maintaining Your Machines," you will learn about persistent state software as a way to help secure desktop computers against privacy issues between multiple users and also help secure the machine against viruses and other malicious software. In a nutshell, persistent state software returns the computer to a predefined state that you set. Between users, then, all of the personal information and files that are left on a computer by the previous patron are erased, and the machine is clean again for the next user. This software can generally be put on laptops but cannot be put on tablets. If you are loaning tablets, you will need to figure out a method for cleaning and clearing these devices each time they are returned to the desk so that the next patron does not accidentally access the personal data of a previous patron.

When touring one large library that did check out tablets, the library clerk explained how they cleared the tablets of personal data and settings once the tablet was returned. They told me that their reference staff cleans the data off the tablets at the reference desk, by hand, "when they don't have anything else to do." So, in other words, the reference staff gets a stack of tablets from the front desk, which have been checked in, and sits at the reference desk hitting "Clear Data" over and over again on each tablet and examining the tablets *by hand* for any installed apps or other problems that need to be cleared.

Not only is this wildly inefficient, it is nonstandardized (not all tablets may be cleared in exactly the same way); staff may miss something that they should delete, and it requires a large staff of people who apparently don't have anything else to do. Obviously, this is not a solution for a small public library. Staff in small public libraries interested in a mobile device loaning program may want to look at loaning devices upon which persistent state software can be installed, which allows the machine to be wiped of personal data automatically each time it is rebooted or shut down. This will make a huge reduction in the amount of time staff members have to spend maintaining the program.

Maintaining mobile devices, especially tablets, can represent a serious investment in time for the small librarian. If you don't have the time to maintain a program like this, you should be honest about it. Again, once a program like this is started in your library, your patrons will expect that program to continue indefinitely.

However, it is possible that such a program won't have to continue indefinitely; more and more people are getting mobile devices, even among persons near or at the poverty line, and as a result there is a shrinking demand for such "loaner devices." Even during my time running my second laptop checkout program, there was a noticeable drop-off in the number of people requesting to check out a laptop, to the point where the numbers perhaps don't support continuation of the program. But don't gamble on such a change. If you aren't prepared to continue the program for at least as long as you are employed at the library, don't start it.

HOW TO START A MOBILE DEVICE CHECKOUT PROGRAM

So you've decided to bite the bullet and start a mobile device checkout program. Where do you begin? The first thing to do is decide *what* you are going to loan. Are you intending to loan tablets? Laptops? EReaders? Some combination of different devices? For the sake of argument, let's say that you want to start a small laptop loaner program.

Obviously, the first step after deciding what you want is obtaining the actual devices. Make sure that you follow appropriate procurement procedures (Chapter 12, "Procurement"), including going out for bids on the devices if necessary, and keep inventory records for the devices (see Chapter 7, "Inventory"). Make sure that once the devices are received they are appropriately labeled so that it is clear the laptops belong to your library. Label each laptop in a couple of locations, both obvious (the lid of the computer) and not so obvious, such as taking out the battery and putting your library name inside the battery compartment.

Once you feel that you've labeled things appropriately, the next step is to determine *where* the laptops will be stored when they are not in use. Consider that, when not being used, you are probably going to want to charge the laptops, so someplace with readily available electrical is a must-have. The laptops will need to be relatively secure if stored away from the public or be stored in a locking case if stored out where the public can access them. A spare room or staff area is an ideal location.

Many companies will try to sell you on fancy "laptop carts" that have built-in charging and are superbly mobile. They are often seen rolling around in school districts, although they aren't completely without precedent in the public library sphere. The short version is that unless you plan to move your service area on a regular basis you should skip the cart and save your money. Any standard shelving with access to electrical will be fine for storing the laptops. Single-face steel library shelving works very well, and the open-frame design of the shelving lends itself to routing electrical cords back and forth.

The next challenge with setting up a laptop storage area is securing the charging packs and power strips that tend to slide around. You may be familiar with Velcro as the stuff that fastens toddlers' shoes, but it comes in all sizes and strengths, including something called "industrial," which comes on a roll and has a release pressure of approximately 10 pounds. This ensures that charging packs and the like stay in place, but it also makes them mobile and able to be removed from the shelf if necessary.

After setting up the location where you intend to store the laptops, the next step is to work up the details of *how* the laptops will be checked out. A few of the many questions to consider are as follows:

1. Will the laptops be checked out for in-library use only, or can patrons take them home?
2. What kind of security measures are in place to ensure a patron does not walk out the door with one?
3. What are the care requirements for your laptops, and how do you make sure the patron respects those?
4. What will your procedure be if the patron damages a laptop?
5. How will you know if a patron damages a laptop if they don't tell you so?
6. Are you willing to loan other devices, such as mice and charging packs?
7. What are the penalties if a patron fails to follow your guidelines for use?
8. Is there an age restriction on who may use the laptops?
9. Are there types of patrons who are not allowed to use the laptops?

All of these questions are open to your interpretation and there is no right or wrong way to pursue determining the answers. You will want to make sure that your library board of trustees stays informed throughout this procedure development process, as they are ultimately responsible for services such as this one, and they will probably want to give input. In some circumstances, the board may want to create a policy or modify an existing one to address laptop use.

In an example scenario, the following decisions were made:

1. Laptops are for in-library use only. They are not to leave the building.
2. Patrons must present both a library card and a photo ID to use the laptops.
3. All patrons checking out a laptop must be over 18 years of age; however, it is allowed for an adult to check out a laptop and allow their minor child to use it.
4. Patrons are presented with a sheet of rules and must sign and date to acknowledge the rules each time they check out a laptop.
5. Patrons are not allowed to borrow the charging packs, as insurance against them taking a laptop out of the building (within eight hours, the laptop would be dead and be unable to be recharged).
6. Patrons are responsible for the laptop at all times while checked out and they must return the laptop directly to a library staff member.
7. Failure to abide by these rules will result in the patron receiving a note on their account indicating they are no longer allowed to borrow laptops.
8. Failure to return a laptop when requested or by closing time will result in the entire cost of the laptop being charged to the patron's account, subject to review.

In addition to this, staff members needed to be trained on how to check out the laptops properly and fill out their portion of the rules' signature sheet. Staff members were also shown how to check in laptops and inspect them for damage before returning them to the storage area to be charged. Staff members were generally enthusiastic about loaning the laptops.

There are a few things to remember about a mobile device loaning program. First, you will have a procedure in place for what to do with a damaged laptop, but you may never have to use it. Patrons generally take an astonishing amount of care when they are entrusted with such a device. It is worth including on the rules sheet in bold type how much the retail cost of the device is. It helps patrons to understand that it is expensive equipment and that they should exercise some care when handling the devices. Second, be careful of your own security devices! If you have the magnetic-style security gates and the machines that "thump" (desensitize) each book to check it out at the circulation desk, DO NOT UNDER ANY CIRCUMSTANCES get the laptop closer than six feet to your desktop security device. This means you will need to put the barcode to check out the laptop somewhere else, such as on a separate 3×5 card. If you get the laptop too close to your security device (which is essentially a giant magnet), it will damage or destroy the laptop.

Finally, you will want to rehearse everything several times before the go-live date for checking out mobile devices. Have staff members practice coming to the desk, pretending to be patrons wanting to check out a device, and have other staff members fill the order. Then reverse the roles so that everyone gets a chance to think through the process of checking out and checking in the devices.

A mobile device checkout program, such as a laptop checkout program, is an excellent way to get patrons interested and excited about technology and to serve patrons who may not have access to such equipment on their own.

In our enthusiasm to serve our patrons, we are tempted to imitate every aspect of a library much larger than our own. However, a larger staff can support a greater range of services, and a mobile device checkout program is one such service that should be implemented only if there are sufficient staff to keep and maintain such a program indefinitely and if there is a budget to replace the devices when they reach the end of their useful life. Regardless of checking out the devices, it is imperative that all public libraries provide some form of wireless Internet access, if at all possible. The core educational and recreational services that the library provides to patrons now demands that wireless Internet access be available to those patrons.

CHAPTER 6

Your Software Arsenal

Nothing is more frustrating than trying to nail down a technology issue that refuses to reveal itself. A suspect computer will work fine for weeks, then randomly throw up a blue screen of death. Staff complains, the machine is rebooted, and it works fine again, this time for three days. Reboot the machine again, and it goes for a whole month. Then there are three days of continuous problems, and then no problems again for a week.

You get the idea. Sometimes, the only things that can help track down an issue with your machine are some outside diagnostic tools. This chapter will explain some of the most commonly used tools and describe how they can help you stay on top of any potential IT issues.

Open source is a term that means that the programming code that makes up the software (the source) is available for anyone to inspect and modify. Generally, open-source software comes with a type of license that allows it to be distributed for free.

The vast majority of the software listed here is freely available. It is open source and presented under various types of open-source licenses. Many software packages are now made available in an ISO format. CDs usually can hold no more than 700 MB and DVDs can hold up to 4 GB, so choose your disk based on the size of the ISO file you are trying to burn. For what it's worth, you can burn a CD image onto a writeable DVD, but not the reverse.

An **ISO** (pronounced ICE-O) is a bit-by-bit data copy of a disk designed to be burned directly onto a blank CD or DVD.

A **megabyte** (MB) is a measurement of a quantity of data. It is approximately 1,000,000 bytes. A **gigabyte** (GB) is approximately 1,000 megabytes.

The reason that software is burned directly onto a DVD is because many of these diagnostic tools are designed to be boot disks.

A **boot disk** is a removable disk such as a CD, from which the computer can automatically operate when the machine is started. When a boot disk is present, the computer will ignore the operating system on the primary hard drive (such as the Microsoft Windows operating system) and instead load an operating system from the boot disk.

To use a boot disk, you simply stick a disk in the appropriate disk drive and then reboot the computer. The computer should automatically detect the disk and run the software from it. In the unlikely event that your computer skips checking the disk drive and goes straight to loading from the hard drive, look for a boot order option in your BIOS/CMOS setup screens. This will tell the computer that you want it to check the DVD-RW drive first for a bootable disk before attempting to boot from the hard drive.

Free programs out there allow you to burn these ISOs to a USB flash drive and be able to boot directly off the USB flash drive the same way you would with a CD. You are welcome to experiment with various programs and methods designed to do this. However, because ISOs were intended to be burned to a disk, that is the method we will cover here.

Free programs for burning ISOs:

InfraRecorder (www.infrarecorder.org)
FreeISOBurner (www.freeisoburner.com)
IMGBurn (www.imgburn.com)
Active@ ISO Burner (www.ntfs.com/iso-burning.htm)

Website addresses and other information are subject to change. Links may go dead or entire software packages mentioned in this book may be abandoned or may disappear entirely. A Google search will help enormously in trying to track down software if something does go missing.

InfraRecorder

www.infrarecorder.org

InfraRecorder is my recommended program for burning various downloaded ISOs to CDs or DVDs. Unlike the large and unwieldy Nero burning software and other commercial products, InfraRecorder leaves virtually no footprint on your hard drive or in memory. Initial installation generally completes within two to three seconds, and you are left with a simple program with six buttons, one of which is "Write Image." Simply click "Write Image," then select your .iso file from your computer and click the "Burn" icon to complete the process. It's that easy. It staves off a whole host of compatibility and licensing issues with commercial burning software.

THE FUNCTIONS OF THE SIX INFRARECORDER BUTTONS

Data disk—creates either a CD or DVD data disk.
Audio disk—creates a CD audio disk that can be played in standard CD players.
Video disk—creates a DVD that can be played in standard DVD players.
Write image—burns an ISO image from the computer hard drive to a CD or DVD.
Copy disk—copies a CD or DVD to another CD or DVD. This can be used even if you only have one disk drive.
Read disk—this creates an image file (such as an ISO) from a CD or DVD and saves it to the computer hard drive.

DBAN

www.dban.org

THIS IS NOT A DIAGNOSTIC TOOL. Short for Darik's Boot and Nuke, DBAN has been around for a very long time. DBAN does one thing—wipes (erases) hard disk drives in computers. This is extremely helpful when you need to simply clean a machine and start all over from scratch, or you want to erase all of your data before disposing of a machine. DBAN includes wipes with varying levels of security, from Quick Erase all the way up through various military-grade wiping routines. **CAUTION:** If you put this on a USB flash drive to boot, unless you remove the flash drive at the correct moment, DBAN will detect the drive and literally wipe itself out. That's why you need to always put DBAN on a CD rather than a flash drive.

Memtest 86+

www.memtest.org

Memtest86+ also does only one thing. It simply runs a continuous test on your computer's memory and provides you with the results. The information provided can be quite overwhelming, but basically lots of red numbers and errors mean that you have either a bad memory stick or, at the very least, need to reseat the memory in your computer. If you get errors, remove all the memory sticks from your computer, then put just one of them in and run the test. If that stick passes, try the next one. Repeat until you've found the culprit. There is no "stop" to this program; you simply remove the disk from the drive and turn off the computer by pressing the power button. Despite the name, it does work with both ×86 and ×64-based processors.

A **memory stick** (also called a memory module or RAM stick) is a small rectangular circuit board that plugs in perpendicular to the motherboard of your computer. The memory stick contains several RAM chips that provide the computer with some amount of memory (common values today are 2 GB and 4 GB). Memory sticks are centrally located on the motherboard and are one inch tall. They can be released and removed by pressing down on locking tabs located on either end of the stick. To reinsert, press the stick into place in the slot and snap the locking tabs closed. Memory sticks are "keyed" so that they will only fit into the slot one way. If the memory stick will not go in, flip it around and try again.

×86 and ×64 are known as **processor "architectures."** The simple explanation is that programs written for an ×86 processor, called 32-bit programs, may or may not work with a newer computer with an ×64 processor. Conversely, 64-bit programs designed to run on an ×64 processor will not run on an ×86 processor. Some 32-bit programs, such as Memtest86+, are cross-compatible, meaning that they will run happily on both types of architectures.

Ultimate Boot CD (UBCD)

www.ultimatebootcd.com

We're fortunate to live in an age where you can fit a lot of stuff on one disk. Ultimate Boot CD is a huge group of individual utilities tied together with a hierarchical menu. Once you select a specific utility, it sets the program to run, and then you usually have to restart your computer to get back to the main UBCD selection screen after the program is complete. UBCD provides the following broad categories of utilities:

BIOS—these utilities allow you to examine and potentially change BIOS data. **Warning:** It is important that you fully understand what a BIOS is and what it does before attempting to use these utilities. Chapter 4 covers BIOS in detail.

CPU—these utilities that deal with the processor of the computer.

HDD (hard disk drive)—these utilities allow you to diagnose and make changes to the computer's hard disk drive.

Memory—these utilities allow you to diagnose issues with the computer's memory.

Others—these utilities are miscellaneous programs such as antivirus scanners and a few other disaster recovery tools.

Peripherals—these utilities allow you to diagnose problems with various computer peripherals, such as the keyboard, mouse, video card, CD/DVD drive, and printer ports.

System—these utilities allow you to either (1) determine information about the hardware inside and connected to your computer or (2) allow you to "benchmark test" the speed of your computer as a whole to determine if it is not performing as intended.

The **hard disk drive (HDD)** is located inside your computer and is the primary storage area for data and files on your computer. Data remains on the hard drive even when the machine is powered off.

Within each category, there may be subcategories that define the utilities even further. For example, in the hard disk drive (HDD) category, there are subcategories for utilities dealing with boot management, data recovery, device info and management, diagnosis, disk cloning, disk editing, disk wiping, installation, and partition management. These will be discussed in depth later.

The main page of www.ultimatebootcd.com, titled "Overview," has a complete listing of the programs and utilities included on the Ultimate Boot CD. You can click on any of the utilities to go to the individual home page and get information about that particular utility.

A word of caution: Some of the utilities on this disk can do serious damage to your computer if you do not completely understand how they work and what purpose they serve. It's not that these programs are malicious; they are just designed to be used by people that know how to use them. For example, the "Disk Editing" utilities are for *complex bit-by-bit edits of hard drive data*, not for other types of editing. Not understanding how a disk editor works means you'll quickly end up with either corrupted data or a corrupted hard drive.

The following are my recommendations for use of this disk by non-professionals:

BIOS: Most of these utilities are designed to either reset your BIOS passwords (if set) or clear your customized CMOS data entirely. I'm not aware that there's any potential to actually wipe your BIOS programming, but use these at your own risk since the BIOS is critical to the functioning of your computer.

CPU: These are diagnostic utilities which are designed to "stress" your computer processor (in a good way) to determine if there are any problems with the processor and to benchmark the speed and quality of the processor—completely safe.

HDD/Boot Management: This section contains utilities which edit how your computer boots from the hard drive and which operating system is loaded. **Stay far away from this one.**

HDD/Data Recovery: These utilities are meant to help you recover data from an unbootable drive. There are also a couple of password-blanking utilities. Make sure you know what the various utilities do before you use them. Use Google to find a description of the individual utility prior to launching it.

HDD/Device Info and Management: This section will tell you information about your hard drive and provides some management functionality. Many of these programs will tell you if there are errors or issues reported by the built-in SMART reporting on your hard drive—generally safe to use.

HDD/Diagnosis: This set of utilities lets you diagnose and test various types of hard drives. You do need to know the manufacturer of your hard drive so you can select the appropriate utility. This may require you to take the cover off your computer and look at the label on the drive or simply try a few utilities till you find one that works. Completely safe, although one or two utilities do offer you options to "fix problems," which you should avoid.

HDD/Disk Cloning: This section contains programs that let you copy one hard drive to another. Pretty much useless unless you have more than one hard drive installed in your system. If you do have more than one, most utilities ask you to select the "source" drive (the one with data on it) and the "destination" drive (the one without). Don't get these two mixed up or you'll lose all your data and end up with two completely blank drives! Generally there is no need to use this section, so avoid it.

HDD/Disk Editing—AVOID THESE: These utilities let you edit the hard drive bit by bit. These are for security experts and the super techy only; there is no conceivable reason you'd use these.

HDD/Disk Wiping: Exactly as stated, these utilities let you wipe (erase) one or more drives completely. These include DBAN as one of the utilities. *Safe to use only if you understand and are comfortable with what it will do.*

HDD/Installation: These are mainly utilities for much older computers that needed to have hard drives "installed" using software. **Leave these alone.**

HDD/Partition Management: Partitions are logical dividers on your hard drive that make the computer believe, effectively, that more than one disk exists on a single physical device. *Unless you understand partitions, these are not safe to use and could destroy your data.*

Memory: This section contains a litany of different memory diagnostic tools. Completely safe to use.

Others: Here you'll find utilities that don't fit into any other categories. They include two antivirus scanners (f.prot and clamAV) and a program called kon.boot that allows you to temporarily bypass Windows and OSX password screens. There's also an instance of FreeDOS here if for some reason you need the plain old C:/> prompt. Generally safe, but pay attention.

Peripherals: Utilities in this section are intended to test other devices on your computer such as the keyboard, mouse, video card, CD/DVD drive, and printer ports. Completely safe to use.

System: These utilities detect hardware connected to your computer and provides other system information. They are a group of valuable diagnostic tools and completely safe to use.

Like medical doctors and the Hippocratic Oath, the gist of using the Ultimate Boot CD is this: "First, do no harm." If you're simply having a problem recovering one file, don't go using utilities that could scramble data or erase the hard drive. On the other hand, if your hard drive is completely unbootable and you've given up hope of recovering the data, you can afford to be a little more heavy-handed with the utilities in a last-ditch effort. Unless you modify the BIOS, the worst you'll have to do is wipe the hard drive and start completely from scratch.

One final note, there is a version of the Ultimate Boot CD for Windows, called UBCD4WIN (www.ubcd4win.org). It contains a different set of utilities designed to run under Windows to diagnose the same types of problems as mentioned with the UBCD. Personally, I tend to prefer UBCD over UBCD4WIN because sometimes, even if you can boot into Windows, the Windows OS itself can be the problem you're experiencing. I like to take the operating system completely out of the equation when diagnosing hardware problems with the computer. If everything comes up clean, then I can boot into Windows, knowing that it must be a software issue with the machine.

Windows System Repair Disk

(operating system built-in utility)

OK, so this one's not technically free. You have to have a valid Windows software license, and the best recovery utilities only began appearing with Windows 7 and above (for another method that's more universal for recovering Windows, see Chapter 4, "Troubleshooting the Individual Computer"). You do have to create this rescue disk while the operating system is in good working order, but once you do, it is universal and can be used to recover any computer with the same version of Windows. You will need a separate disk for 32-bit systems and 64-bit systems.

To create the disk in Windows 7 (Windows 8 is similar), go to Start Menu, then Control Panel, then System and Maintenance, and then click "Backup and Restore." Click "Create a System Repair Disk" on the left side of the screen, then follow the simple directions to create your disk. Once the disk is created, in the event of an issue with Windows that prevents it from functioning, you simply insert the repair disk like any other and reboot the computer to load from it. When you boot from the DVD, a simple menu will guide you through all of your possible options, up to and including wiping and reinstalling Windows (which of course will cause you to lose your data). Look before you leap and Google more information if you are unsure what a particular utility does. For what it's worth, in Windows 8 the utility is called **Create a Recovery Drive**, and the default media for the recovery disk is a blank flash drive instead of a DVD.

ANTIVIRUS PROGRAM BOOT DISKS

No particular website or name of a particular disk is given in this section, because there are so many, and they all work wonderfully. Really, all you need to do is Google "antivirus boot CD" or "antivirus boot disk," and you'll find that nearly all of the major vendors provide some sort of a free antivirus that you can boot from CD in the event of an emergency. This antivirus does what all do; it looks for bad files and malicious configurations and restores or removes these problems as appropriate. Again, virtually all of the major third parties, such as Kapersky, Avira, and AVG, have a rescue boot CD available for free. There is no right order in which to run these CDs. If you believe your computer has been overrun by a virus and now won't boot (or the virus prevents you from using Windows correctly), simply burn and then boot from one of these CDs and scan away. If one CD doesn't get it, try the CD from another vendor. Do note that there are some viruses, such as versions of CryptoLocker, which have **NO** removal. These viruses encrypt your files, and unless you have the key, you cannot decrypt the files again. The only options are to either decrypt the files (there are removal utilities for some but not all versions) or wipe your computer and start over. The files aren't recoverable while CryptoLocker has the files encrypted.

Encryption is the process of mathematically re-coding the contents of a file based on formula. The formula operates by taking an input string of characters (known as a "key") and using that key to calculate what the new value of each bit in the file should be. The short version is that if you do not have the key you cannot decrypt a file and restore it to its original, usable state.

AND MORE . . .

Many, many more types of boot disks, all with specific functions, are available for your use, and the vast majority of them are free. Be suspicious if you actually have to pay for these utilities, although you might consider making a donation to the programmer via his or her website if you find the utilities useful. To name one example, **Trinity Rescue Kit** (trinityhome.org) is a slightly more automated version of many of the functions found on the Ultimate Boot CD. Which you use is a matter of preference; Ultimate Boot CD offers the most control over when and how each utility runs. In short, there is probably a boot CD out there that will allow you to identify a problem that prevents a computer from booting and may in some instances be able to fix it for you.

A wide variety of software is available to be burned directly onto CDs and DVDs. These are designed to be used in a "rescue boot" situation in which the computer loads utilities from the disk prior to attempting to use the operating system on the hard drive. Boot disks allow you to check most every component of your computer and identify many problems that would otherwise remain hidden. It is important to have at least a few of these disks on hand to minimize downtime in the event of a true emergency.

CHAPTER 7

Inventory

So you've averted the immediate crises that were identified when you first triaged the IT for your organization. You may have even had a chance to work on some lower-priority, "shine and polish" tasks. Before you get too used to the routine, however, you need to take a complete inventory of all of the IT equipment in the building. Some of the reasons for this include the following:

1. In the event of a catastrophe such as a power surge that destroys some or all of your equipment, the insurance company is going to want a list of the equipment that was destroyed, including serial numbers and specifications.
2. If you are suddenly approached by your supervisor and told that there is money available for IT, you need to have a list of projects ready to avoid looking like you aren't interested in the funding.
3. It helps you to keep track of warranties so that, if a computer does go bad, you can tell at a glance if the company might service or replace it.
4. It helps with planning for an upgrade cycle. Assuming you are allowed to purchase computers every year or every few years, you need to know which ones are the oldest, have the lowest technical specifications, and are most in need of replacement.
5. An inventory works in combination with a network diagram (covered in Chapter 10). Having a complete inventory on hand can be extremely helpful when planning changes or upgrades to a network.

The word inventory often conjures up visions of warehouses, "logistics," and those little scanner doodads that some retail employees carry around to check store inventories. An inventory, for any reasonably sized organization, doesn't need to be that complicated.

There is no one right way to do an inventory, and your primary mission is to place essential information about each device in a format that is readily accessible and easily readable.

HOW TO NAVIGATE MICROSOFT EXCEL

The first thing you need to decide is what program you'll use to keep track of an inventory. I don't recommend a plain Microsoft Word document unless your inventory is very short, because it makes it difficult to compare down a field (comparing the manufacturing dates of all the computers you own, for example). Microsoft Word, however, is great for adding long-winded "appendices" to the inventory for specific machines. For example, if you have notes explaining that you had to request a replacement hard drive from the manufacturer, all the documentation on that may best be kept in a Word document where there is room to spread out, rather than a tiny column in a spreadsheet.

Most frequently, people who create inventories use Microsoft Excel. That's right—Excel, the spreadsheet program. Some of you who have had training in Microsoft Office may say, "But wouldn't a database in Microsoft Access be better suited to the task?" The answer is yes, technically. But Access is probably the least user-friendly of the big five Office Suite programs (those being Word, Excel, Outlook, Access, and PowerPoint). Microsoft Access databases have some amazing abilities to run "queries" and return just exactly the information you're looking for. They also have "keys" and ways of making sure that no two rows are ever repeated. But on the flip side, you also have to consider that Microsoft Access can be a pain to use, unless you've had some significant training. The idea of fields in databases and keys and all of those other things that some people take for granted doesn't come naturally. It's a different way of thinking that requires time and effort to get right. On the other hand, most people are used to Excel rows and columns as either a traditional spreadsheet or as a makeshift way of organizing records.

My point is, if Excel works for you, go for it, as long as you recognize what Excel can and cannot do. Excel, for the most part, lacks some of the advanced sorting and querying functions that are present in Microsoft Access. This usually isn't a problem as long as your inventory isn't fifteen pages long (which means you probably have several hundred computers and are way outside the scope of this book anyway). And if you do ever feel that Microsoft Access is a better choice, there is some support for turning a spreadsheet into an Access database. See the Microsoft Access help file or Google for more information on this.

My suggestion is Excel for three reasons, even though you understand databases and know how to use Microsoft Access:

1. Excel is quicker and easier to navigate, even after having had training with Microsoft Access.
2. You can share your inventory file with people who have no training in Microsoft Access but can navigate Excel.
3. It prevents issues with people who have no access to Microsoft Access. Excel and Word are by far the top two programs and the ones that virtually every person with a Microsoft-based machine is likely to have available. You could also simply turn your completed inventory into a PDF and distribute it that way, but that prevents others from manipulating the data on their own.

In this book, Excel is used to show you how to construct a basic computer inventory. Please don't e-mail me about how I'm using the wrong program for the task; I know. But this is the program I expect that the layman IT person will be happier with in the long run.

AUTOMATED INVENTORY PROGRAMS

About this time, you've been in the inventory section of this book long enough that your subconscious brain is starting to think, "Do I really need to go around to every computer and get the information individually? Isn't there some way to automate this process?" The answers are "yes" and "yes, but I wouldn't recommend it."

A plethora of programs on the market today, both free and otherwise, purport to automate the inventory process. Possibly the best well known of these is a freely available program called Spiceworks Desktop (www.spiceworks.com). More than just a simple executable program, Spiceworks Desktop is actually operated via a web browser which queries files on your local machine. To do this, Spiceworks Desktop installs a complete database schema and associated services that run every time you start your computer. In plainer English, unless you're running a fairly high-powered machine, expect that you might notice some drag on your boot times once Spiceworks Desktop is installed.

This chapter will only discuss the automated Spiceworks Desktop program. There are actually two parts to Spiceworks; the database program called Spiceworks Desktop (mentioned earlier) and the Spiceworks website, which allows you to chat with other techs on a variety of different message boards. The latter is highly recommended as an excellent way to stay in contact with other IT people.

When you run Spiceworks Desktop, it scours your local network for other connected devices. Once it comes up with a list of devices to inventory, Spiceworks requests that you enter **credentials** (usernames and passwords) for each device. Depending on your network setup, one set of credentials may suffice for an entire group of devices.

Spiceworks Desktop purports that if all of the credentials are entered properly it should be able to inventory 100 percent of devices on your network in a matter of minutes. In practice, on a variety of different networks, even with credentials that are accurate, I have never succeeded in obtaining over a 70 percent inventory success rate on the first pass and never over an 85 percent success rate after multiple attempts.

Many supporters of Spiceworks Desktop will question my technical abilities, my setups, and even my integrity at this point. But this book is aimed at nontechnicians who have been thrust into the IT spotlight and, on top of that, people who are running single-person IT shows. You won't have time to be trying to Google why Spiceworks Desktop is choking on valid credentials.

Granted when Spiceworks Desktop does inventory accurately, the level of detail on the inventory is quite astounding. But on the other hand, it is probably more information than you are likely to need. If you do need that information for a particular machine, in a small organization you can pull it directly from the machine when you need it. The most detailed thing needed is the make and model of a particular card or chip, and that only when the computer has malfunctioned anyway, and you will probably have it open on the test bench where you can easily find those numbers.

Spiceworks Desktop has value in a large organization, and if someone was to distribute a base image (that is to say, an exact bit-for-bit copy of the hard drive) to 600 identical machines, they would all show up in Spiceworks Desktop on the first try. But that's not normally the way it works in small organizations, and so it is not recommended for our purposes here. Feel free to tinker with Spiceworks if you like, but realize that you may work with it for weeks and never get all of the devices on your network to appear in the inventory.

For our needs, automated inventory programs are simply going to be more trouble than they are worth. In the next edition of this book in a few years, that may all have changed. At this time, you cannot "just download this program, run it, then skip to the next section of the book." But there's some definite value in visiting each machine to determine individual configurations:

1. You can visit each machine and be able to immediately determine which (if any) is physically malfunctioning.
2. You're able to make observations about the machines such as load times and responsiveness.
3. You can place a personalized inventory tag for your organization. This is handy for identifying every piece of equipment with a short serial number that does not change and is not reused.
4. You are able to determine the purpose of each machine within the organization.
5. You are able to at least get a casual idea whether some machines may need to be relocated.

CREATING THE EXCEL SPREADSHEET

At this point, we return to constructing our makeshift Excel inventory. The first step in this process is to determine what kind of information you and your superiors, and perhaps the insurance company, want in a computer inventory. Ask your supervisor if there is anything specific he or she would like to know about the machines. Ask your organization's insurance representative what kind of information he or she would need about the machines if one or more of them were destroyed in a catastrophe. You might be surprised at the type of information that he or she will ask for.

Take all of this into account when you input the information into your spreadsheet. The first row is for the column headings of each type of information, such as make, model, and year of manufacture. Each row below that is a record for one computer in your organization (see Table 7.1).

Provided you don't have other more expansive needs, use the following column headings:

1. Make (manufacturer) of the computer
2. Model of the computer
3. Serial number or service tag of the computer (service tags are simply short serial numbers for some computers, see later)
4. Date of purchase
5. Date of installation
6. Type of warranty (three-year, next business day on-site, etc.)
7. Warranty expiration date
8. Processor type and speed
9. RAM
10. Notes

Table 7.1 A Sample Computer Inventory

No.	Make	Model	Serial No.	Purchase	Install	Warr. Type	Warr. Exp.	RAM	CPU	Notes
1001	Dell	Optiplex 740	FDM30XA	4/30/2009	6/11/2009	3-year NBD	4/30/2012	3 GB	Intel Core2 Duo 2.6 GHz	Purchased with Grant
1002	Dell	Optiplex 740	FDM30XB	4/30/2009	6/11/2009	3-year NBD	4/30/2012	2 GB	Intel Core2 Duo 2.6 GHz	Purchased with Grant
1003	Dell	Optiplex 620	RJ63YA3	3/13/2006	unk.	1-year	3/13/2007	2 GB	Intel Pentium 4 2.0 GHz	
1004	Dell	Optiplex 620	RJ63YA4	3/13/2006	unk.	1-year	3/13/2007	1 GB	Intel Pentium 4 2.0 GHz	

Starting from the top, the make and model of the computer are universally important. This has been somewhat supplanted by newer manufacturer's websites that allow you to look up a specific computer by the serial number or by the service tag; if you have the tag, the site will identify the model for you. Serial numbers and service tags are unique to each computer; no two computers are manufactured with identical serial numbers or service tags. Serial numbers are long numbers (often 10 digits or more) that are frequently located on the back or top of the case and are also frequently recorded *incorrectly* due to the length of the number. Service tags are much friendlier versions of serial numbers that accomplish the same purpose—identifying an individual computer among all the computers that have been manufactured by a particular company. Service tags are a short combination of letters and numbers, which can often be found on the top or back of the computer case.

The company that leads the way (in my opinion) in web-based lookup of service tags is Dell Computer. Dell provides a short service tag that is an easily identifiable combination of letters and numbers for each computer in lieu of full serial numbers. You simply visit the Dell support website and the main page requests that you enter a service tag in order to retrieve more information about a computer. When you enter a service tag, you're immediately directed to a customized portal for the computer that you specified. The machine manufacture date, hardware configuration at the time it left the factory, warranty information, manuals and other documentation, and software updates are all available from this portal, and all are tailored to the specific computer service tag that you've entered. If you've inherited a bunch of Dell computers without knowing any of the warranty statuses, the support website is the place to obtain that information. Dell seems to have taken exceptional care with its portal to ensure it is as user-friendly as possible.

Other manufacturers also provide a similar serial number lookup service on their websites, but the type and quantity of the information that is presented varies. The primary problem with some other manufacturer support sites is that they can be quite difficult to navigate.

The computer's date of installation will have to be estimated unless you know for certain when the computer was installed. If you can't find a date of purchase, you may just have to add a couple of weeks from the manufacture date. In other cases, you may just want to leave this field blank, especially if you have a confirmed date of purchase.

That last two bits of information you'll need to know about each machine are the amount of RAM that is installed and the processor speed and type. These two items will help you determine when it is appropriate to upgrade the machine.

Formerly, it was necessary to record how large a hard drive the machine had. This has become less and less relevant as storage sizes have jumped and cost has dropped. It is now not uncommon to see a 500 GB hard drive come as standard equipment on a newly purchased machine. That is far more than the average user in a public library environment will need (at this point in history, anyway), and so it is generally no longer necessary to record this information. You still may want to do so in specific situations, such as when carrying out the inventory of a file server. The rest of this chapter will show you how to retrieve this information from an individual machine if the manufacturer's website doesn't provide the information.

HOW TO FIND INFORMATION ABOUT YOUR COMPUTER

Several places provide information about the computer, both inside and outside of the Microsoft Windows operating system. For now, we're going to focus on software-based retrieval of this information. Remember, if all else fails, you can always physically open the case and look at individual labels to record how much memory and what type of processor is in the machine. But there's no need to go pulling parts out of a car if a metaphorical service manual will tell you what's installed instead.

The first stop in the quest to obtain information about your computer is the BIOS/CMOS setup screen. When you first start your computer and your computer says something like "Press F2 to enter Setup," that's the screen we're talking about. Press whatever key the computer tells you to press, about once a second, until the computer enters the setup screen. If you aren't sure what key to press, just turn on your computer and mash the F1, F2, Tab, and Delete keys at random. Chances are good it's one of those four.

The very first screen you come to will generally provide you with information about the computer itself; listed here could be your processor speed and type, as well as how much RAM is currently installed. If you're really lucky, it might list the RAM by slot, which tells you not only how much RAM is installed but also (conceivably) how much room is left if you wanted to add some memory. Depending on the setup screen, it may also list identifying information about your computer such as serial number and service tag (if any).

Beyond this default screen, other information about your system is also available on other screens within the setup utility. For example, you may find how many and which types of drives are installed on the computer (hard drives, DVD-RWs, etc.), the make and model of these drives, and other information, such as the storage capacity of each. Some computers will also provide you with make and model information about other devices inside the machine, such as the network chip. It isn't common to find this information in the setup screens, but sometimes it is there.

To exit the setup, follow the directions provided on-screen to exit. If you haven't actually made any changes to the setup that need to be saved, you can also simply press Ctrl+Alt+Del to restart the computer. Let the computer load into Microsoft Windows.

Your next step is to visit some of the built-in features that come with the Windows operating system. These functions are available with every version of Windows currently in use, as of this writing. However, there's always something new on the horizon, and right now Microsoft Windows 10 has already been released. The information provided here can, and no doubt will, change in subsequent editions of this book.

But for now, our hot key to success is to press ⊞ + R. That brings up the "Run" dialog box on all versions of Windows. Though there are other ways to access the functions we're going to cover, this one is by far the quickest.

In the Run dialog box, type "msinfo32" and press Enter. This brings up Microsoft's system information tool, which provides you with a huge amount of information about the computer you're currently working on. It's very easy to navigate; simply pick a category and a subcategory on the left-hand side and wait for a brief moment while Windows retrieves the information. One of the most relevant screens is the very first one displayed by default: the System Summary. From this screen, you can obtain information about your version of Windows, the make and model of your computer, RAM, processor speed, and more. Spend a little time in the system information tool and you'll see it's a powerful resource, especially if you are working in tandem with another more experienced professional to diagnose a problem.

After you're done with the system information tool, bring up the Run dialog box again, type "Control Panel," and press Enter. This is simply a shortcut to the Windows Control Panel that we all know and love. Newer versions of the Control Panel include a search tool in the upper right-hand corner of the window, which is a huge boon for tech personnel since with every new version of Windows it seems like Microsoft is determined to move around, add, or eliminate something from the Control Panel. From the search bar, search for **Device Manager** and press Enter, then click on the result for Device Manger. Device Manager is a utility that allows you to view all of the devices connected to your system in a hierarchical fashion. It also allows you to view information about those devices, though the amount of information provided will vary with the device. Device Manager can, in addition, tell you if a device is malfunctioning (yellow exclamation mark icon) or not detected/not present (red "x" icon). On top of this, by double-clicking on any device, you get an easy-to-navigate set of tabs, which allows you to search for and potentially update drivers for a device that either doesn't have the appropriate drivers or doesn't have any drivers at all.

Finally, there is a little bit more system information available elsewhere in the Control Panel. From the search bar, type "System" and then click on the *main* (green) link for the System settings, not any of the other more specific links underneath. This will bring up the "View Basic Information About Your Computer" screen, which provides you with information about the processor, RAM, activation status of your version of Windows, and also (depending on the manufacturer) some basic support contact information in the event you're having a problem. On newer versions of Windows, there is also a "Windows Experience Index," which purports to tell you, based on your machine's configuration and specifications, how awesome or not awesome your Windows experience is likely to be. Don't even bother with this gimmick. The self-evaluation process to assign a number can take upward of five minutes (sometimes upward of ten) and still only gives you a number that the technology industry at large refuses to acknowledge as valid or even useful.

The set of utilities described earlier should provide you with more than enough information to complete a basic inventory of the computer. Any more detailed queries (like the specific make and model of network device if the Device Manager doesn't provide this information) will probably require opening the machine itself and recording the numbers and other information from the chip.

These utilities are quick and easy to access, so once you get a rhythm going, inventorying all of your computers really shouldn't take you that long. The information it provides and the decisions it will help you make are well worth the investment of time that you make at the beginning to ensure everything is accurate.

A computer inventory is essential for making rational, well-informed decisions about upgrades and replacements, as well as providing valuable security in the event an insurance claim needs to be made. Simple, user-friendly utilities, both outside and within Windows, make this task easy and worth the time required. Once an initial inventory is completed, it requires only a commitment to update the inventory and keep it accurate when adding, upgrading, or removing machines from service.

CHAPTER 8

Networks and Networking

Among the most intimidating pieces of equipment in your library are those having to do with networking. Comprising a stack or rack of square and rectangular boxes, flashing lights, and exotic varieties of cables protruding from every possible opening, network equipment is the heartbeat of a modern IT operation in an organization of any size. This chapter is intended to walk you through the basic components of a network setup, from start to finish. Along the way, we'll be documenting each component and how they connect and relate to other components in the network. At the conclusion of this chapter, you'll have what's known as a "network map."

THE NETWORK MAP AND IDENTIFYING NETWORK COMPONENTS

A **network map** is simply a drawing of the way your networking equipment is connected. Think of a network map as the picture you'd get if you were able to lay all the networking components flat instead of stacking them up. Imagine they are spread out on a football field. What you would see in the Goodyear blimp is a bird's-eye view of how all of your network components are related to each other and where all of the cables go—that's a network map. A network is generally made up of

- a network rack,
- a patch panel,

- a DSL or phone line, a TV cable, or a thin fiber connection,
- an internet modem, a router,
- a firewall,
- a network switch (sometimes several),
- an uninterruptible power supply (UPS),
- a wireless router or wireless access point, and
- Ethernet patch cables, which connect all of the components together.

We will work through each of these components, stopping to describe its function and then documenting it.

Begin by locating the network equipment itself. Generally, this will all be located in one place, perhaps in a back room away from patrons to prevent tampering. Depending on the size of your organization, your equipment may be mounted to what is known as a **network rack**. A network rack is simply a steel frame to which equipment can be mounted. This provides the net effect of "stacking" all of the equipment vertically while each individual component remains parallel to the floor. Racks are ideal for a variety of reasons, but don't sweat it if you don't have one. The chapter reads as though you did have a network rack, but the network setup and connections are the same with or without one.

Always start your network map by locating your incoming Internet line. The way this looks will depend on the type of service to which your organization subscribes. If you get Internet via DSL, look for an incoming phone line. If you subscribe to cable Internet, look for a round cable that looks like a TV cable. And if you are one of the lucky folks that has a fiber connection, look for a thicker cable (thicker than a power cord) that doesn't match the other cables on the rack. Depending on how your rack is set up, the thick black cable might enter a **demarcation** box (demarc for short) and turn into a pair or more of thin wires right before it attaches to your rack. Other types of Internet service, such as cable and DSL, will not have a demarcation box.

In any event, the first stop for the incoming Internet cable will be a small box, which is usually eight inches or less square. This is your **modem.** The Internet Service Provider (ISP) supplies you with this piece of equipment. The job of a modem is to translate the signals from your ISP into something that your network equipment can understand and translate and transmit data from your network equipment back over the ISP's network. The name *modem* comes from the days in which Internet and other data services were provided over Plain Old Telephone Service (POTS) lines. Your modem would dial the ISP and speak to it in a series of rapidly **mo**dulating pulses (which sounded like static to anyone picking up the phone). The modem would then **dem**odulate the pulses coming back from the ISP and change them back into data that your computer could understand.

Today, the actual function and look of these modems varies widely, and they no longer "dial in" to the service. Most frequently, they are used to maintain a constant and stable connection between you and the ISP and to make all of your equipment play nicely with their equipment. In addition, the modem often gives the ISP the ability to make some basic remote diagnosis if you are having problems with Internet service.

Since you've found the modem, take a pad of paper in hand, start at the top, and draw a line to indicate incoming Internet. Near the top, connect this line to a square. Label this square "DSL Internet Modem" or "Cable Internet Modem" or whatever equipment you are using to access the Internet.

The modem will most likely connect to the rest of your network equipment through an Ethernet cable. As mentioned in a previous chapter, Ethernet cables are the standard cable used to allow your computers to network to one another. This is the type of cable that is more commonly just referred to as a "network cable," and that's the term that will be used for the rest of this chapter.

The network cable coming out of the modem to your network equipment will generally attach to another box, which may vary widely in size, depending on its age and functions. This box is your firewall. Draw a square below the modem on your pad of paper, label it "Firewall," and draw a line between the two.

Firewalls sound very much like they belong in an epic fantasy card game, and their function in the data stream to and from the Internet is no less epic. The **firewall** (Figure 8.1), inspects all of the data passing to and from your network and determines which data should be allowed to pass through from the Internet to your internal network and which data should be allowed to be sent from your network to the Internet.

This data flows through your network in small chunks, called **packets**. The purpose of packets is simple: Sending small amounts of data at a time allows the computer to save time if one of those chunks of data is damaged or missing. For example, say you were to write down your entire life history by hand (a lot of data) and mail the only copy of it to a friend across the country. That would be awesome, unless the letter got lost or was damaged in transit. Then your friend wouldn't receive anything readable at all, and you'd be stuck having to write out the whole thing and send it all again. As a result, you choose to send your friend a bunch of letters, each with a certain number of pages from your life history (a much smaller amount of data). Then if your friend determines he's missing pages 36–40, he just asks you to resend those particular pages instead of the whole story. It saves a lot of time.

Data works in exactly the same way. If a packet is damaged or missing, the network equipment that received the data asks the sending equipment to try sending that packet again. Since the packets are small, it takes a very short time to re-transmit the missing data, and this avoids having to resend the entire file.

Firewalls inspect packets coming in from the Internet to your network and leaving your network for the Internet. If the firewall determines that a packet is malformed, potentially malicious, from an untrusted source, or otherwise dangerous, the firewall simply drops that packet before it ever reaches your network. On the other hand, if the packet is well formed and from a trusted source, then the packet is given permission to enter and is allowed through the firewall to the rest of the network.

From this point forward, if you have a network rack, most equipment on your rack will generally be a standard 19 inches wide. While the width is standard, the height of

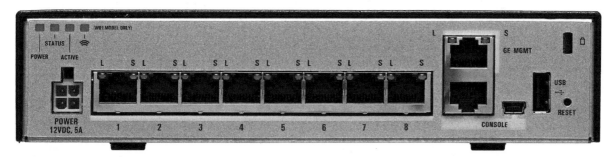

Figure 8.1   A firewall. Courtesy of Cisco Systems, Inc. Unauthorized use not permitted.

Figure 8.2   A router. Courtesy of Cisco Systems, Inc. Unauthorized use not permitted.

equipment on the rack may vary. Equipment that is approximately two inches high is referred to as taking up one **rack unit**, or 1RU for short. Equipment twice that height is 2RU, and so on and so forth.

Next, look for a cable that exits the firewall and connects to another box. This box is most likely your **router**. Think of a router (Figure 8.2) as performing the same functions as your local post office. Local post offices take large carts of mail from a single source (say an over-the-road truck) and sort them all so that they are ready to be delivered to the appropriate addresses. Similarly, a router takes all of the incoming data from the Internet and sorts it based on which computer on the network requested the data. Conversely, the router takes outbound data from many different computers and packages and transmits it so that it can be sent back through the firewall and modem. Modems don't always like to talk to more than one device, and a router solves that problem. In reality, the router is a gateway; when provided data from the Internet, it sorts the data and passes it to multiple connected computers via a network switch, described later.

Because the routing functions are so closely tied with the work that the firewall does, it is very common now to see firewalls with integrated routing components. Put another way, the firewall can support configuration for multiple networks and all other major tasks that a stand-alone router would provide.

Return to the paper on which you are drawing your network map. Go back to the square that you labeled firewall. If your router is separate from your firewall, draw another square below your current drawing and label it "router." Again, draw a line between the two, which represents a physical connection. Conversely, if your firewall and router are a single unit, simply erase the "firewall" label and change it to "firewall/router."

Next, find the network cable coming out of the router box. Follow it. If your network is typical for a small organization, the cable you follow will terminate into a wide box with a bunch of network cables coming out of it. Depending on the size of your network, this equipment could have anywhere from eight female network connectors (called **network ports**) all the way up to 48 ports.

> **Port gender**, which is the practice of identifying ports and plugs as either male or female, is adopted from more traditional mammalian anatomy terms. A plug with prongs or pins is known as a male connector. A port or socket designed to receive one of these connectors with pins is known as a female connector. Gender changers are small adapters that are designed to remedy a situation in which both ends of a required connection are of one gender type.

You may also have several of these boxes that are connected to one another, providing even more ports. This device is known as a **network switch** and its function is distinctly separate and yet just as important as the router. A network switch (also just known as a "switch") **polls**, or requests, information from devices as they are connected and keeps track of the ports to which they are connected (Figure 8.3). In an example scenario, you have a network switch with only four ports. Port 1 is connected to the computer at the front desk, port 2 is the computer on the cataloger's desk, port 3 is a computer in the library workroom, and port 4 the connection back to the router. The switch polls these devices for information as they are powered on in the morning and finds out which one is connected to which port on the switch. The switch then memorizes this information and builds a table in memory to keep track of these locations. If you turn on a connected computer, for example, that computer is polled and the table is updated almost instantly with the new information. If you shut down a computer, the switch detects that the client has disconnected and updates the table accordingly.

Switches then, in our post office metaphor, are like the local postman. A packet of mail leaves the post office, and the router (sorting room) has determined that it is bound for a specific computer. However, only the local postman, who is already familiar with the neighborhood and has the house addresses memorized, is able to get that packet to the correct address quickly and efficiently.

Historically, before network switches were commonly available, there was a networking device known as a **hub**. Hubs performed no memorization of computers or addresses; when a packet of data came through from the router, intended for a specific computer, the packet was duplicated by the hub and broadcast to every port. Using our post office metaphor, the local postman made multiple copies of the same letter and ended up with one letter accepted and three copies marked as "return to sender," because they were not intended for the house on the other end. It goes without saying that this is an extremely inefficient way of doing things, and switches were a vast improvement on the data flow. While hubs are as dated as the Pony Express, your library may still have one or more

The easiest way to determine if you have a hub or a switch is to look for descriptive wording on the case. Some will say "hub" or "switch" right on the front. If you aren't that lucky, Google the model number of the device and you should be able to determine quickly if you are dealing with a switch or an older hub. If you happen to have identified a hub that you are still using on your network, **consider upgrading it to a switch as soon as possible**; the upgrade is generally as simple as unplugging the old device, unplugging all the network cables from the front, and then plugging it all into the new device. You will immediately see increased speeds on your network from this upgrade.

In order to provide more network ports, often several switches are linked together with physical cables, a process known as **uplinking**. On some older switches, a specific port was required to be used to link two switches together—usually port 24 or 26. There was also a button labeled MD/MDX, which had to be physically adjusted to tell the switch if the port was being used for uplinking or not. Hopefully, your network switches no longer have a port 24 or 26 with a manual MDI/MDI-X button. Modern switches do away with this complication; they can be uplinked from any port on the switch and automatically negotiate the uplink and begin communicating with the other switches in the stack, without any button-toggling. However, if you still have older switches, you may have an

Figure 8.3 A network switch. Courtesy of Cisco Systems, Inc. Unauthorized use not permitted.

MDI/MDI-X button. Generally, one switch should be set to MDI, while the other switch to which it is connected should be set to MDI-X. However, this may vary. See the user manual that came with the switch or look online to determine the requirements for your specific model of network switch.

Usually, uplink connections are made with a regular network cable. Sometimes if your network is very well put together, this cable will be a different color to show it is an uplink cable. If your network is extremely well put together, you may actually have a separate fiber-type cable that links one switch to another. My network definitely does not have these, but realize they are a possibility, especially if the initial installation of your network was done all at once by a commercial company.

Once again, return to your network map and draw boxes below the firewall/router representing each one of your network switches. Connect them with lines representing physical cables where appropriate. If you did not already do this during the inventory phase, label each switch with a letter to differentiate them one from the other (i.e., Switch A, Switch B, etc.).

After examining the switches, look to see where all of the network cables leaving the switch route to on the rack. Usually, they almost all go to either the top or the bottom of the network rack, where they terminate in another set of ports much like the ones on the network switches. These are "ports on a board" and are known as **patch panels**. A patch panel's job (Figure 8.4) is simply to make it easy for you to make adjustments on your network. Just as there may be several network switches, there may also be several patch panels on a single rack as necessary to serve all of the network cables in the building. Patch panels differ from other networking devices because they are not powered; they are simply a convenient way of making connections between two cables. If you don't have a patch panel, you will probably have a bundle of long Ethernet cables and connectors coming out of the wall, which you then have to sort out, untangle, and plug into your switch individually. A patch panel, on the other hand, allows you to use a short Ethernet cable (known, not surprisingly, as a **patch cable**) to connect a port on the patch panel to a port on the switch or other networking equipment. On the back side of the patch panel, there are special, semi-permanent connectors called punch-down connectors that let the Ethernet installer connect ports on the front to the much longer Ethernet cables that travel through the walls of your building to various computers and other devices. If for **some reason you don't have a patch panel, consider getting one installed**. As you become more proficient with your network, you will be glad the convenience exists.

Normally, patch panels are not directly included on a network map, but since this is your network, feel free to add them if you like. Usually, there is a separate document informally called a **patch panel map** with squares that represent each port on the patch panel and notes as to which devices or ports they serve elsewhere in the building. You may have to create this document if it does not already exist.

Finally, you need to consider how your network equipment is receiving power. Is it plugged into a series of power strips or surge protectors? If so, that's OK for now, but there

Figure 8.4   An Ethernet patch panel. Courtesy of Cisco Systems, Inc. Unauthorized use not permitted.

is a safer, better option available. The next level of equipment beyond simple surge protectors is known as an **uninterruptible power supply**, or **UPS**. A UPS device (Figure 8.5) plugs into a standard-voltage wall outlet. Then you plug the various power cables from your networking equipment into the UPS, rather than into the wall. The UPS makes sure that no voltage surges, spikes, brownouts, or blackouts cause damage to your sensitive network equipment.

The secret to a UPS is an internal battery that is constantly charging. In a normal scenario, power from the wall not only charges the UPS battery but also passes through the UPS to power your networking equipment. The UPS has very sensitive circuitry that monitors the status of the wall voltage. If a voltage surge or drop occurs, the UPS reacts in a fraction of a second and switches the networking equipment over to steady battery power until the problem with the line voltage has passed. When it has passed, the UPS will automatically resume providing line voltage from the wall to the networking devices.

The switch between wire and battery happens so quickly that the networking equipment doesn't even know the difference. Most UPSes, however, also have a USB port. If you connect this port via a USB cable to your computer and install the software included with the UPS, you'll be able to get statistics on how reliable your wall power is, the health of the battery, and more. Even though it doesn't have to do with the "data" side of things, a UPS is as much networking equipment as any other device on the rack. *If you don't have your networking equipment protected with a UPS, you're taking a very big risk.*

That's really just about as complicated as small-organizational networking gets. Now that you've learned the basic building blocks of a network, you can start to get a concept of some more specialized network equipment that is constructed off these principles.

A **wireless router** is a device that combines routing functions, a network switch, and a wireless radio all into one package. Depending on the type of wireless router, some firewall functions may also be included. The wireless router takes an incoming Internet connection and routes it to various computers attached to it via a wireless network. The switching principles in a wireless router are all software based (except for the Ethernet ports on the back of the router, if there are any). The wireless router memorizes which devices are connected to the wireless router and how to find and communicate with them, effectively performing the same function as a network switch.

This is why wireless routers are so popular in the consumer market. As far as the end user is concerned, they are literally plug-and-play. You simply plug an Ethernet cable from your Internet modem into one end of the router and plug the router into the wall. The network is constructed and configured automatically. Modern wireless routers even walk the

Figure 8.5 An uninterruptible power supply (UPS). Courtesy of APC by Schneider Electric. Unauthorized use not permitted.

consumer through the steps required to create an encrypted, private network, as opposed to an open one. For the home market, these devices truly are one-stop networking for the entire house.

A **wireless access point** (Figure 8.6), on the other hand, is simply a device that uses a wireless radio to grant computers access to an already existing network. Think of it as a wireless switch without the routing capabilities. If you plug a wireless access point directly into an Internet modem, nothing will happen, because the wireless access point lacks the ability to route data from the modem. A wireless access point is simply a gateway through which wireless devices can access an existing network.

Figure 8.6 A wireless access point. Courtesy of Cisco Systems, Inc. Unauthorized use not permitted.

To enhance the ability for wireless networking radios to be placed anywhere, many wireless routers and access points now support **Power over Ethernet (PoE)**. Rather than get power from a wall outlet (which just uses a wall-wart transformer to lower the voltage anyway), these devices can take power directly from a set of unused wires in the Ethernet cable so that when the device is plugged into the Ethernet it is automatically powered and ready to go. Of course, the network switch port on the other end of the cable must support transmitting power to PoE devices. If the switch does not support PoE, data transmission will theoretically be unaffected, but the PoE device itself won't operate unless it is also plugged into a wall outlet. Support for PoE still varies by make and model of network switch. Look for ports labeled as such or (if you're lucky) the entire switch labeled as supporting PoE.

The benefits to PoE are obvious. Since Ethernet is considered low voltage (such as telephone wire) it can be run anywhere inside a building without the many restrictions that common electrical wiring has, as to where and how it may be run. Many times, for example, wireless network devices are placed high up on a column or wall for the best signal coverage. Unfortunately, there typically aren't outlets available in those locations. To solve this, you would simply connect the Ethernet cable to a PoE switch on the other end in the networking room and the device would take off and run just as if it was plugged into a wall outlet.

OTHER MYSTERY NETWORKING EQUIPMENT

The devices mentioned earlier may not be the only ones you have connected to your network rack. It would be naive to assume that no one has a device attached to their rack that they "just aren't really sure about." Following are some steps you can take to look up unidentified equipment:

1. Google the manufacturer and model number to determine what type of device it is. You may also be able to download a manual for the device from the manufacturer's website. You'd be surprised how nontechnical the language actually is in some of those manuals.
2. Determine if the device is actually connected to anything on the network! This isn't actually as crazy as it sounds. On more than one occasion, my examination of a network rack turned up a spare device (such as a cable modem), which is literally powered on but with nothing attached to it. At some point, the network completely bypassed the device, but it was never removed from service.
3. Call in a favor. Find an acquaintance with more networking knowledge than you have to figure out what the purpose of the device might be. Post a picture of the device online to IT discussion forms such as Spiceworks (www.spiceworks.org) to see if anyone can enlighten you. Ask your supervisor for any and all network diagrams or other diagrams that they have regarding the IT setup of the building.
4. Call in the hired experts. If all else fails and you really can't figure out what something does, call in a more seasoned professional. When you're done drawing your network map, there shouldn't be any "mystery boxes" with unknown functions or connections. Since everyone is sensitive to budgets, obviously you want to avoid the paid solution

until last. However, you also need to know how your network works in complete detail as part of emergency planning. If you get a call sometime that the network has gone down, the culprit may very well be the mystery box that you'd always previously ignored. Learn what it is before it is too late.

Originally, a suggestion five was going to be "unplug it and see what happens," but this isn't really a recommended approach. Even in noncritical applications, you could really cause problems by just taking a component out of the middle of your network structure at random. In addition, you're assuming that when you plug the device back in, it's going to come up and restart exactly the way it worked when you powered it off. With unknown devices, you have no idea what might happen. If you do unplug something to figure out its purpose by process of elimination, you do so at your own risk and against the recommendations of this book.

WHAT ABOUT COMPUTERS?

Are end-use devices such as computers and printers considered part of your network? Absolutely! Should you put them on a network diagram? Possibly, depending on the scope of your services and how big a paper you are working with. For example, in a campus network map, where the central network serves individual buildings, the core network is illustrated and then there are "backbone" lines leading to icons that represent each individual building; all the computers in a particular building are on the same network leading from this backbone. Then another network map is created for within the building, which illustrates the core networking equipment within the building and any sub-networks, if they exist. This network map may then have backbone lines leading to icons that represent individual floors or sections of the building. One more high-detailed network map may detail each section of the building and show individual computers connected to the switch on that floor. So for large organizations you actually have a series of network maps that increase in definition as you focus on a specific area of the network.

For a small- to medium-sized organization (usually under fifty machines), depending on the space available, it may be worth putting the core network down the center of the page, and to the side illustrate each individual workstation, then detailing which switch it connects to on the core network. In other cases, especially with multiple floors or defined areas, it may make sense to put these on another more detailed network map.

Remember also that you should have a port map that tells you which patch panel ports are connected to which equipment. You could also code it such that it explains both the workstation it serves and the switch to which it is patched on the network rack. This would prevent having to put individual workstation connections on your network diagram.

Whatever you decide to do, it is important to post a completed network map (including all levels of detail) and port map next to your network rack. That way, if a third party has to walk into the situation cold (like you did) and try to figure out the network, they'll be able to quickly determine how the network is set up and be able to diagnose the point of failure (which is presumably why they would be there).

Insurance companies also appreciate these maps, as it gives them an idea of the kind of equipment you are using. Submit it to them along with your inventory sheet (see Chapter 7, "Inventory"), to ensure that you have protection in the event of a power surge or other catastrophe that destroys equipment.

Even though you can make a network diagram by hand with a ruler, there are programs available that make this task significantly easier. Network Notepad (www.network notepad.com) is software that can be thought of like a specialized paint program. Network Notepad starts with a blank canvas and allows you to insert "icons" that are graphical representations of devices on your network. Network Notepad comes with some of these icons by default, and more can be downloaded for free use from Cisco Systems. See the Network Notepad website for details on doing this. Once the icons are inserted, you can connect them together with lines that represent physical network connections. Each icon (called an object in Network Notepad) can have properties assigned to it, such as a name, IP address, and description. This makes it easier to tell not only what a device is but also its role on the network. Network Notepad is an excellent tool to have in your IT kit. It is available in both free and full-featured pay versions.

Now that we know the basic equipment, here is a quick checklist of what you will need to order if you have no network in place:

- A DSL, coaxial TV cable, or thin fiber connection
- An Internet modem (often provided by the Internet Service Provider)
- A router
- A firewall
- A network switch
- A UPS
- A wireless router or wireless access point
- Ethernet patch cables, which connect all of the components together

Having covered your network map, it's time to troubleshoot. Here are the things to do when you have a problem with your network.

TROUBLESHOOTING A NETWORK-LEVEL ISSUE

Perhaps one of the first things you noticed on arrival in your new position, especially if it was dark in the server room, was the multitude of flashing and blinking lights on the network rack. Each one of those lights has a specific meaning, and we're going to go over some of the major ones. A term you'll need to be familiar with in this section is **power cycling**. Power cycling is just a fancy term that means you should unplug a piece of equipment, wait one minute for the memory to clear and activity to stop, and then plug it back in. Unlike power cycling a desktop computer (mentioned in a previous chapter), there is no need to hold the power switch after the device has been unplugged. Simply unplug, wait, and then plug back in. Most network equipment does not have an easily accessible (to you) reboot function, and it is just as happy with the power being removed and restored to reboot it as long as you wait at least one minute to clear the memory and avoid a power surge.

YOUR FRIENDS "LINK," "ACT," AND "PWR"— AND YOUR ENEMY "ERR"

It's funny. Networking equipment is standardized to the width, depth, type of power connector, and type of Ethernet connector. But for some reason the manufacturers have never gotten around to standardizing indicator lights on various pieces of equipment. While the lights required for equipment obviously vary based on what the equipment does, some of the lights that indicate statuses common to every piece of equipment are located in all manner of different places, depending on the manufacturer and even the model. If there is a standard, it is within a brand, such as Cisco or HP Procurve. But even within those brands, the lights can travel from one place to another, depending on the type of equipment or the size of network it is able to handle. Therefore, what we'll discuss here are some of the major indicator lights that generally show up on each piece of equipment and where they might show up.

1. **Power (or PWR)**. It is common across virtually all equipment and perhaps the easiest to diagnose. If your equipment has no power light (and for that matter no other lights), it either isn't turned on via the switch in the back (if there is one) or it isn't plugged in at all. Check your power source and all the connections and try again. Try switching to a different outlet. Check the power indicator light on the power supply if there is one. Don't assume the equipment itself is lost until you have no other options. A blinking power light generally indicates the equipment is starting up (since there is no monitor to indicate this). A steady power light means the equipment is powered and ready to go.

2. **Activity (ACT)**. This light indicates that there is data flowing to and from the equipment. Sometimes there is an ACT light for each port; sometimes there is just one for the entire piece of equipment (such as with cable modems). Sometimes this is also labeled "data," though this isn't as common. An ACT light should generally be rapidly blinking in an irregular fashion; the light usually blinks more or less in time with the data that is received from the port. If an ACT light is dark, there is no data being received from the port; check your Ethernet connections. If the ACT light is blinking regularly about once per second, the equipment is using the port to try to negotiate a connection to equipment on the other end. If it doesn't resolve within a few minutes, something is usually wrong with the equipment on the other end. If the ACT light is lit steady, something is probably wrong. Try power-cycling the equipment and see if the problem persists. If it does, there may be an issue with that device, but double-check the equipment on the other end first, as well.

> **Mbps** and **Gbps** are short for Megabits per second and Gigabits per second, which are measures of the speed at which data is transmitted from one piece of equipment to another. 1 Gbps is approximately equal to 1,000 Mbps.

3. **Link (LNK)**. Link lights on equipment are very versatile. In the most basic form, they simply indicate a good connection with equipment on the other end. Because this can also be a feature of the ACT light, sometimes equipment foregoes LNK lights entirely. When the equipment (such as switches) do have LNK lights, the lights

generally appear one per port and indicate simply that the port is connected or indicate the speed at which the port is running. This indication will vary by make and model (see your manual), but one example may be that the light is amber if the link speed is 10 Mbps, green if the link speed is 100 Mbps, and flashing green if the speed is 1 Gbps (1,000 Mbps). Some equipment also features dynamic link lights in which pressing a button on the front of the equipment puts the link light in different "modes" and allows it to display additional information besides the link speed. For example, one switch I have used has modes as follows in order of the button press:

- Link status—shows if the port is connected or not.
- Link speed—shows if the port is transmitting and receiving data at 100 Mbps or 1 Gbps.
- Power over Ethernet—shows if the port is providing equipment on the other end with PoE.

Of course, it goes without saying that if the LNK light is not lit something is wrong and there is no connection. Either the Ethernet is not connected or the equipment on the other end is not even providing power to the network port.

4. **Error (ERR)**. This light is usually amber in color. It is much less common than it used to be and most often seen on equipment supporting older high-speed connections. Normally all (data) errors are handled internally by the network equipment itself, making this light unnecessary. Some dynamic Link lights (see earlier) can duplicate the function of this light. Some older equipment simply separates this light out from the others so you can see how frequently data errors are occurring.

5. **Alarm (ALM)**. This light is usually red (not amber) in color. Again featured mostly on older equipment maintaining a permanent connection, ALM would indicate that the equipment on your end is not communicating with the equipment on the other end for some reason; the loop between the two is broken somewhere. This could be either bad equipment or a bad wire or a bad terminating connection on one or both ends. Most networking equipment you'll deal with does not include this light.

6. **1,2,3,4, etc.** These are simply LNK lights that have the port numbers they represent rather than the word LNK.

7. **Wide Area Network (WAN)**. On some equipment that maintains a link to the larger world (such as a router), there is WAN light that indicates the status of the connection to the WAN. If your internal network is thought of as the Local Area Network (LAN), the WAN is the higher-level network that your network connects to. In all but the most complicated of cases, the WAN connection will be the Internet, and most times the Ethernet cable that plugs into the WAN port will come directly from your Internet modem.

8. **Those *@$!! icon lights on wireless routers**. For some reason, companies decided that on some home and small business wireless routers the consumer couldn't understand the meaning of simple words such as "Link" and "Activity." Instead, these helpful words have been replaced with a series of only marginally helpful pictograms that for most folks usually requires a trip to the instruction manual, at least at first. Here's a common codebook for them:

- Globe = WAN light
- Dot with radiating lines = Status of the wireless radio
- 1–4 = LNK lights for the wired Ethernet ports on the back of the router.

- Power light = varies by model
- WPA light (or similar) = indicates that your encryption is working. The value of this light is questionable, but it makes you feel like a boss when you set one up at home and this light comes on.

PUTTING IT ALL TOGETHER

So now that we've had an elaborate tour of common lights, how do we put it all together? What do we do when there is an actual network issue?

The first thing you should do, before a network issue even exists, is create a "lights" chart for yourself. On a lights chart (which you may construct however you like), you record each piece of network equipment that is on your rack. Then next to each piece of equipment, you list all of the lights and what they are doing under normal conditions (for example, PWR light steady, LNK light amber, ACT light rapidly blinking). That way, when there is an actual network issue and you believe you have it narrowed to a specific piece of equipment, you can refer to the chart and see if the indicated lights vary from a normal condition for that equipment. If they do vary, you may have found your culprit.

The first step in diagnosing an issue is to grab that chart and then determine what services are not available. Are you unable to print to the network printer? Is there no Internet? Are you unable to access files on your network drive?

Network equipment is designed to be very stable and not prone to errors, so determine there are no mitigating circumstances. Check to make sure the issue is occurring on multiple computers or, in the case of inability to access files, check to make sure the server appears to be operating properly. Check the link lights on the back of computers to make sure there is actually a connection to the equipment in the network room. Check lots of things, but when you finally suspect network equipment, head to the network room.

Depending on who you ask, there are different methods for this next process. Some people work from the head of the network at the Internet connection down to the final switch that connects computers to the network. My choice is to work backward, starting with the switch that is connected to computers that are experiencing issues, and then work my way back up to the WAN connection at the head of the network. As you gain more experience, you may be able to jump directly to the suspected equipment, but for now the methodical approach is going to be the best.

Start with the switch that connects your computer equipment to the network. Compare it with your lights chart. Does everything appear to be normal? Are there any amber lights that shouldn't be there? Are the activity lights blinking rapidly? If not, what are they doing? If you determine that the switch might be the issue, power-cycle it. If the issue doesn't happen again after the power cycle, make a note of the issue, time, and date for future reference. That way, if it happens again in two weeks you can perhaps begin to suspect a faulty piece of equipment. If it doesn't happen again, it may have simply been a transient issue. Sometimes changes in line voltage can cause equipment to crash (although a good UPS unit should filter this out, and if you don't have one, shame on you! See the section of this chapter on network equipment). Line voltage is notoriously tricky, and a standard 120 V outlet can measure anywhere from 113 V to 130 V depending on a variety of factors. And despite that wide range, you only visually start to notice "brownout" in your lights at about 105 V. Equipment can be affected long before your eyes realize what's going on.

If the switch is functioning properly, work your way up to either the next switch to which it is uplinked or your firewall/router. Firewalls and routers generally run more advanced software and are ever so slightly more prone to crash. Check the firewall and router lights. If they aren't indicating correctly based on the lights chart that you made, power-cycle them and look again. Finally, work your way up to the Internet modem. Examine the lights on that device and double-check that they are acting normally. If you have problems accessing Internet throughout a building, the Internet modem (and/or the service it is connected to) should be highly suspect. If you're confident that it's the Internet service provider's equipment acting up, call your Internet service provider and say so. Don't take "no" for an answer. Identify yourself as the IT administrator for the building and tell the representative that you already have recorded how the equipment is supposed to act under normal conditions and that the indicator lights are not showing a normal state of the equipment. If the representative seems unsure or hesitant, you may need to ask to be transferred to a higher level of support.

As for making networking equipment perform more advanced tricks, this chapter will stop short of introducing you to router or firewall programming simply because the software and methods can vary so greatly. Cisco, for example, has 500+ page books on the software (iOS) that's used to program their firewalls and other equipment. To successfully program the equipment, you will need to read and follow the user manual that came with the equipment. This is usually provided on a CD or available as an online download. And if you aren't sure, ask for help. Unfortunately, especially with the higher-level professional networking equipment, the software can be somewhat touchy. If you enter an incorrect command, for example, it may take effect immediately and bring down your network, and you're stuck trying to navigate in a foreign operating system with no idea of how to reverse what you just did. When it comes to programming these devices, it is better to be safe than sorry and hire the work done. If you insist on programming your own equipment, at least do it during a low-demand time when you won't have people breathing down your neck if something goes wrong.

Hardware-based network equipment is actually fairly easy to diagnose, assuming that you begin with a functioning network and make some notes about how it is operating before you encounter a problem. Don't be afraid to work with network hardware. It is designed to be very stable and rebooting equipment is as simple as a power cycle. More advanced network management, such as Cisco iOS software programming, is perhaps best left to a network specialist.

CHAPTER 9

Networks, Servers, Clients, and Addressing Servers and Clients

Network hardware is actually only one piece of the networking puzzle. It is equally important to introduce you to the concepts that govern the network devices you will actually use on a daily basis.

SERVERS AND CLIENTS

In terms of PC hardware, there are two main roles—server and client. **Client** computers are the end-user machines that you work with every day. They are the "regular" computers that sit under or on your desktop or perhaps are even bolted to the back of your flat-screen monitor. Client computers generally have a full-feature processor, storage, and the ability to carry out commands and functions independently from other machines.

Servers are specialized computers that have a more powerful processor, extra memory, and a lot more storage than a desktop client. The server's role is to support the clients by providing file storage, connections to other devices such as printers, user credential authentication (username and password verification), and a variety of other configurable services. In one sense, the transaction between a server and a client is very much like a restaurant. Servers exist to serve the clients, and clients request things from the server. If a connected client (one at a particular table) requested a steak from the server, the server would go to the kitchen (file storage on the server) and retrieve it for the client. Rather than each client trying to hold a full complement of food on their own table, the server holds the food in a central location with much more room and produces the food upon the request of a client. Since the kitchen is larger and better equipped to handle the task than a normal client at a table, this transaction doesn't take long.

Centralized servers provide another benefit, which is that files can be shared among many users, and multiple users (assuming they have permission) can edit a single file. This assists greatly with workflow and collaboration within organizations. One of the primary purposes of "logging in" to the server through a client computer is to determine which files you have permission to access.

Though what was just described is the typical relationship between clients and servers in an organization, there are other models. One example is the **thin client**. In this model, much more of the processing and information is shifted to the server. The desktop client itself has very little processing power, little or no internal storage, and very little memory. When the thin client is turned on, it immediately requests further instructions from the server about what to do next. The server then provides the client with a **virtual desktop**, which is a mini-operating system that allows the user to interact with the server in a familiar environment (such as Windows) on the client, when really the server is providing almost all of the processing. Thin clients are typically characterized by the inability to function independently—that is, if they are disconnected from the server, they will not function. Contrast this with full desktop clients that have storage and can be used independently in an offline mode if they are disconnected from the server. The informal name for a full-featured desktop is a **fat client.** You are most likely to encounter thin clients in a situation where many computers all need to present exactly the same environment to users. Even though your library might benefit from a thin client setup, it is unlikely that you will encounter one; there are some start-up costs associated with the thin client/virtual desktop model, and at this point, it is generally cheaper and easier to buy regular desktop computers every few years than to make the case for the added cost of moving to thin clients.

No matter the model, there are some common roles that are filled by a small business server:

1. File services. Provides clients with network storage, personal network folders (or "drives"), and allows sharing of folders and files among multiple users with appropriate permissions.
2. Authentication. Makes sure usernames and passwords provided by clients are valid and grants permissions for a particular username.
3. Print processing. In this role, a server accepts print jobs from clients, sorts them, and sends them to a central printer as the printer is ready to process them. Many larger multifunction printers, such as the Konica Minolta Bizhub series, now have print servers built in. This means that multiple print jobs from several locations can be sent directly to the printer. In this case, the print processing role on the small business server is bypassed.
4. DHCP server. It provides IP addresses to clients. This is described later.
5. DNS. It assists clients with the resolution of names (such as google.com or public-server.int) to IP addresses. See later for more.

DHCP, DNS, AND IP ADDRESSING

Most of the server roles are self-explanatory. However, two of the roles, DHCP and DNS, are a bit more complicated.

First, you need to understand that every computer on a network, or more precisely every **Network Interface Card** (**NIC**), has two types of addresses by which they are identified. The first type of address is called the **MAC address**.

A **Media Access Control Address** (**MAC Address**) is a permanent address assigned to each network card that is made up of a combination of a number assigned to the manufacturer and a number that varies with each NIC. No two NICs have the same MAC address, and the address is not *supposed* to be able to be changed. Some devices, such as wireless routers, can "clone" another MAC address on the network to help with compatibility issues. For simplicity's sake, assume that every device has a permanent MAC address.

When a client device joins a network, it immediately begins a process of discovery, whereby it sends out requests for information about its position on the network and the network switch or other device to which it is attached. At the same time, the network switch begins by identifying each connected device by its MAC address and memorizes which port on the switch that device is accessible through. Toward the end of this initial negotiation process, client devices such as computers will obtain an **Internet Protocol (IP) address** and also other network settings that allow it to operate on the network. Normally, client devices such as computers are set up to request an IP address by default from a **Dynamic Host Control Protocol (DHCP)** server. DHCP is simply a fancy way of saying that the server will automatically send out network configuration information and assign IP addresses to client devices that request it.

IP addresses are the basic numerical addresses that identify devices found on networks that surround us every day, from your small local network clear up through the Internet itself. When you type in www.google.com to a web browser on a client computer, the computer contacts a **Domain Name Server (DNS)** (in this case, one owned by your local ISP) to determine the numerical IP address that belongs to www .google.com. The DNS sends your computer this IP address, and your web browser stealthily uses that IP address to connect to the server at google.com from then on. Pretty slick, huh?

Your local network server also operates its own DNS, albeit a small one. The local DNS helps by resolving plain-English device names such as PUBLICSERVER and MYPRINTER to the appropriate IP addresses on the network.

Every device on every network that you'll ever use has an IP address assigned to it. To make things slightly more complicated, there are now two types of IP addresses: **IPv4** and **IPv6**. You've probably seen IPv4 addresses before and not realized it. They are a block of four numbers as shown:

aaa.bbb.ccc.ddd, i.e., 192.168.203.120

Whole books have been written on IP addressing. What you should know is that most small networks still use IPv4 and that your network most likely does as well, unless it has been built entirely from scratch in the last six months by a hired professional. IPv6 is coming for internal networks, but right now it is really not necessary. IPv4 and a network router are all that you really need.

In a nutshell, when it comes to IPv4 addressing, you'll probably only ever deal with the last two sets of numbers, ccc and ddd, and you may only deal with ddd. Once you learn what aaa and bbb are for your network, chances are good that no matter what ccc and ddd are aaa and bbb will not change.

The IP addresses assigned to servers on the Internet are all unique. However, internally, there are three "pools" of IP addresses that have been set aside for use by local (private) networks. Wherever you go, you are likely to see some variant on these three IP pools as the internal networking scheme:

10.0.0.0 through 10.255.255.255
172.16.0.0 through 172.31.255.255
192.168.0.0 through 192.168.255.255

So, for example, your network could be set up such that all devices use 10.10.30.ddd. In other words, all of the devices on your network have the same IP address *except* the last three digits of the IP address, which vary depending on the device.

If you have well under 253 devices (consider 0, 254, and 255 reserved), this is probably as complicated as your scenario gets. Pat yourself on the back for understanding how IP addresses are assigned to your devices.

Some networks actually are "split" into two **subnets**, meaning a different IP range is assigned to different parts of the network so that, for example, computers on the public side of the network cannot talk to computers on the staff side of the network.

What you should understand here is that the first three sets of numbers (aaa, bbb, and ccc) *must match* in order for two devices to communicate on the network. If even ccc is changed between two devices, those two devices will not be able to communicate, because the subnet on which the device operates has changed. And if your router, server, and other equipment do not use this subnet, the device with the incorrect subnet will not be able to participate in the network at all.

On the reverse side of things, this trick is often used to separate communication between two sets of devices. One set of devices may have a subnet of 10.10.30.ddd and the other may have a subnet of 10.10.31.ddd. The two sets of devices will not be able to communicate with one another.

It is important to remember, though, that operating two subnets requires two separate network switches (one for each network). In a typical two-subnet setup, you will simply have two physical network switches, one serving each network. A single network switch cannot handle two subnets at once unless it is **Virtual Local Area Network (VLAN)** capable. VLANs are outside the scope of this book. If multiple subnets are something you're interested in pursuing, you are advised to consult with an independent network technician. Two subnets may only "come together" on a single device when that device is designed to sort the traffic, such as with a router or routing firewall. These devices, properly configured, can ensure that the data from both networks do not mingle. For simplification purposes in the rest of this chapter, the example network will have only a single subnet.

To review, a device (such as your desktop computer) powers on, loads an operating system, and requests to join the network. The network switch obtains and memorizes the MAC address of your computer and the port to which it is connected on the switch. The local DHCP server, which is also connected to the network switch, already has the configuration information for your particular network, as well as a "pool" of IP addresses that can be assigned to devices requesting them via DHCP. Your computer requests an IP address and is assigned 10.10.30.102.

This IP address is now **leased**, or assigned, to your client and will remain so until the lease expires. Lease times vary, but usually are at least a day. After the lease has expired, your client computer must again request an IP address from the DHCP server. It may be assigned the same address or a different address if another device has taken the released address in the interim.

In addition to being assigned an IP address, your computer is also given other network configuration information: a subnet mask, a gateway address, and a DNS address.

A **subnet mask** is a rather complicated way of subdividing IP addresses. It is largely outside the scope of this book. In virtually all scenarios you will come across, the subnet mask will be 255.255.255.0. It is important to understand, however, that the subnet mask is *not* an IP address. It is a way of mathematically interpreting the IP address given to your client machine.

A **gateway address** is an address that your client computer uses to access a higher-level network. If, as in our example network in the previous chapter, your incoming Internet is connected to your router/firewall, the gateway address is an IP address that tells your client computer how to contact the router. In order to access the Internet, your computer must know the address of the router from which it needs to request access to that higher-level network. Generally, though not always, gateways are set as the lowest numerical address on a particular subnet, excluding zero. So if your computer address is 10.10.30.102, the gateway address for the router is likely to be 10.10.30.1.

A **DNS address** is the IP address that allows your client computer to contact the DNS server on the network. Generally, your local DNS is hosted by your local server. Name resolution requests ("please tell me the IP address for google.com") are forwarded out by the local DNS to the Internet Service Provider's DNS as appropriate. If your computer cannot contact the local DNS, a variety of problems can ensue, including but not limited to the inability to log into the network and the inability to contact Internet websites.

Static addressing is an alternative to DHCP. In this scenario, you know the configuration of your network in advance and you set your network card to permanently have a particular IP address on the network. You also set the other required information such as subnet mask, gateway address, and DNS server address. The advantage to this scenario is that you always know which devices have which addresses, so tracking down a device with a problem can be less of an issue. On the other hand, you'd better get the configuration just exactly right, because you're intentionally disabling the automated process designed to do it for you. Static addressing can create **IP conflicts** in which two devices on the same subnet are inadvertently assigned exactly the same IP address. In this case, both computers get thrown off the network and neither operates correctly, or at all, until the IP address of one of them is changed to resolve the conflict. By the way, if you happen to assign a static IP address that is within a pool of DHCP addresses available to be leased to clients, the DHCP server detects that the address is already in use and simply skips it when leasing addresses.

Unless you really see a need for static IP addressing, stick with DHCP. It is a lot less of a headache.

Client computers and other devices on a network are supported by servers in various capacities. IP addresses are the fundamental addresses that allow identification and communication of these devices across a network. Most networks are configured using DHCP to automatically assign IP addresses. Having a basic understanding of how IP addresses are assigned will assist in the troubleshooting process, by allowing you to identify problems with network configurations.

CHAPTER 10

A Short Primer on Electricity

When working with computer equipment, it is important to have a basic concept of how electricity works, even if you aren't into installing your own electrical outlets.

Electricity comes in off power lines from a substation elsewhere in your town. These lines, which usually carry in the neighborhood of 4,800 volts (V), connect to a "pole transformer," the big doodad at the top of a telephone pole that looks like an overgrown soda can. If you have underground lines, look for a large green box on the ground that says, "Danger, High Voltage, Do not open." These transformers step the voltage down from 4,800 V (which is needed for longer-distance transmission) to approximately 240 V.

Amps and volts have an important distinction. We're used to saying that high voltage will kill a person. Actually, when we touch a doorknob and get a static shock in wintertime, we're passing on the order of 35,000 V to our skin. **Volts** (V) are a measure of electrical pressure, and the exceptionally high pressure is what's necessary in order for electricity to jump through the air from our skin to the doorknob. Lightning is another great example of high voltage. However, the actual measure of electrical current is in **amperes** (colloquially called "amps" or represented in the SI measurement system with the symbol A). If you think of volts as how hard the water is pressing against the dam, then amperes are how wide the river is (the volume of electrical current). As little as two-tenths of an ampere running directly across the heart can result in cardiac arrest. The voltage doesn't even have to be that great so long as there is enough electrical pressure to pass it through the heart. The difference between the doorknob and the lightning is the number of amperes and volts that pass through your body. With lightning, both the amperes and volts are very high. When lightning strikes a person, it can immediately cause (among other things) burns, seizures, paralysis, cardiac arrest, and potentially death. Static electricity, on the other hand, has high voltage but low amperes, meaning that it is very unlikely to damage your skin but could potentially ruin sensitive electronics.

Modern electrical outlets in the United States deliver approximately 120 V at 15 amperes. Some devices might say that they run on 110 V and not 120 V, but at this level of voltage the difference is negligible. Based on this, you now know that the advice about not sticking a fork in the toaster is sound; 15 A is 150 times the amount required to stop your heart, and with enough electrical pressure that will easily pass through your skin. So the first lesson is: Don't mess with line power, period. Leave that up to a certified electrician. You could kill yourself or set your building on fire, or at the very least, get your insurance canceled if anyone ever finds out you did the work without a license.

Now that we have that warning out of the way, let's go back to where electricity enters your building. Modern electrical service generally includes two 120 V wires and a neutral, the sum total of which means there is 240 V entering the building. Modern electrical service (again a generalization) is 200 amperes (A), meaning there are theoretically a maximum 100 A on each 120 V line. A commercial service for a building may have much more power. This is only an example for a typical residential or very small commercial building.

The power enters your building after passing through at an electric meter, which is a device that measures your total building electrical consumption in kilowatt hours. After entering the building, the service wires go directly into a circuit-breaker box. This box is full of what look like black or gray switches, called **circuit breakers**. Each circuit breaker services one circuit inside the building, which is a section of wiring within the building designed to provide up to 15 A or 20 A and 120 V or 240 V, depending on the breaker. For example, several outlets and the lights for a particular room in the building may be connected on one circuit. Circuit breakers are designed to automatically shut themselves off (called **tripping**) if the amperage demanded by a particular circuit exceeds what the circuit is able to provide. Theoretically, the number of amps you can demand from an electrical circuit is unlimited. The real reason a circuit can't provide more than 20 A, however, is because the size of the wires used to service the circuit won't allow it. If the wires carried any more than this maximum current, the wires would overheat and start a fire. Therefore, circuit breakers are an important component in fire protection. In your circuit box, you may also see 30 A and 50 A breakers. The wires for these circuits are usually dedicated to one device and are much thicker than the standard 15 A wire. There is also a "main disconnect" circuit breaker that effectively turns off power to the rest of the circuit breakers in the box. The main disconnect breaker will be stamped with the maximum number of amperes that all of the circuits in the box can draw at once (usually 200 A or more if it is the main panel).

All this background is to explain the electrical "golden rule" for the IT person. The rule is: DON'T OVERLOAD YOUR CIRCUITS. Just because a circuit breaker is supposed to idiot-proof the electrical system doesn't mean it will prevent a tragedy in every instance. And especially with computers, "tripping" a breaker creates a voltage surge and is very, very hard on connected equipment.

It's easy to make sure you don't overload a circuit. Simply reference your building blueprints (or test during a low-use time) to see which breaker is connected to the outlets that you want to use. See how many amperes are listed on the handle of the breaker (in this example, we'll take 15 A). Add up the amperage of **all** the equipment that will be connected to that circuit and ensure that it does not even approach 15 A. At most, you want 12 A–13 A maximum on a 15 A circuit, to leave a little "wiggle room" for the unexpected. The ampere draw for computers can generally be found on the back label near where the power plug enters the computer (on the power supply). If amperes are not listed, but only watts, simply take the number of watts and divide by the number of volts (120). This will give you the ampere draw of the equipment. In other words, use this well-known formula, based on Ohm's Law: I=P/V, where I is amps, P is watts (the measure of power consumed by the circuit), and V is volts. This formula can also be used to determine the number of watts from amperes and volts or determine the number of volts from amps and watts.

While we're on the topic of overloading circuits, don't abuse power strips. The National Fire Protection Association (NFPA) has codes that state that one "power tap" (that is, a device that turns one outlet into four or six, such as a power strip) is allowed per outlet on a temporary basis. NFPA 1:11.1.4.2 specifically states, "The relocatable power taps shall be directly connected to a permanently installed receptacle." Therefore, you may not "daisy chain" power strips (plug one into the wall for more outlets and then plug a second power strip into the first power strip for even more outlets). You may not use a "cube-style" plug-in multi-tap to plug three power strips into one outlet. You may not plug an extension cord into an outlet and then plug a power strip into the extension cord to extend the power strip's reach. The NFPA really frowns on anything that forces a single wall outlet to do more than it was designed to do for any length of time. In addition, NFPA 1:11.1.4.3 reads, "Relocatable power tap cords shall not extend through walls, ceilings, or floors; under doors or floor coverings; or be subject to environmental or physical damage." In other words, the power strip cord MUST be routed away from foot and chair traffic. Excessive traffic can damage the insulation on the cord and present a shock hazard.

In the United States, power plugs generally come in the "two-prong" and "three-prong" varieties. The third prong (which is round while the other two are slotted), is called the **ground** or **earth** prong. In the event that a wire comes loose inside your equipment and somehow causes exterior components (such as the metal case) to be electrically live, the ground wire (which is attached to the inside of the case) will ensure that the electricity is safely shunted away. In the absence of a ground, the unfortunate alternative would be for you to touch the case and for your body to become a path to the ground for the electricity that has nowhere else to go.

Even when the device is functioning correctly, the grounding pin provides an added protection for electronic equipment. It helps discharge static away from the sensitive components of the device. If you've ever touched a computer case and felt a small static pop, that's a built-up static charge leaving you through the grounded exterior of the case. Failure to ground these types of electronic devices as intended with a grounded outlet could result in static traveling instead through sensitive internal components, which will be destroyed in the process.

Much to the chagrin of the NFPA, adapters are commercially available that allow you to turn a three-prong plug into a two-prong plug. The adapters, nicknamed "cheater adapters," assume that the center faceplate screw on your two-prong outlet is correctly grounded, which in my experience is very rarely the case. If your equipment requires a three-prong outlet, do not cheat and plug it into a two-prong outlet. Not only do you risk destroying the equipment through an ungrounded static discharge, but it is also potentially hazardous if there is an electrical fault with the equipment.

You may, however, plug devices (such as table lamps) with only two prongs on the plug into a three-prong outlet or power strip; these devices do not require a ground and will function happily and safely with either two- or three-prong power outlets.

A basic understanding of electricity will help you to determine where and how to build your technological infrastructure. The primary rules are to know how many amperes are available on a circuit and to not overload the circuit, to use power strips appropriately, to never defeat the third grounding prong for any reason, and to hire a professional to add outlets or perform other electrical work as necessary.

CHAPTER 11

Maintaining Your Machines

Now that everything is calm (okay, maybe not entirely calm, but as close as a one-person show can expect to get), it's time to think about how you're going to maintain the computers (aka the machines) that you worked so hard to get to a functional state. There's a variety of items to consider, choices to be made, and schedules to be set.

UPDATING YOUR MACHINES

The first thing to look at is what might be required to keep your computers up-to-date. This is exceptionally important not only from a security standpoint but also because there are simply some updates that make your computer *perform* better than it previously was able. Updates can correct issues with the way data is processed by the operating system, for example, or modify key components of the operating system (such as the .NET Framework) to work with newer and more advanced software.

I generally divide updates into three major categories:

1. Microsoft updates—this includes everything you would get from the built-in Windows update utility, including updates to other Microsoft software such as Microsoft Office Suite.
2. Antivirus updates—this includes all antivirus definition updates, as well as any software updates for the antivirus program itself, which are received directly from the antivirus provider through the update utility of the antivirus program.

3. Third-party updates—any other software on the computer that needs to be updated from time to time. This schedule may be regular or irregular and includes everything from Java Run-time Environment updates to Adobe Reader updates to driver updates for the computer itself. This may also include updates that control the software-based security of the machine, detailed further along in this chapter.

Microsoft Updates

Microsoft updates are designed to be as automatic and as seamless as possible. Automatic updating is virtually always turned on; if you haven't yet been asked by Windows to turn on automatic updating, then you haven't been using Windows very long. On our personal computers, most of us just say yes, turn on Microsoft update to full automatic (needs no authorization to run), and don't even pay attention to *when* it runs.

However, in a larger organization, it is handy to schedule Microsoft updates for a time when you can maximize the Internet bandwidth available in the building, such as before you open or after you close the doors on a particular day. Because you will be updating multiple computers at one time, the bandwidth requirements can be quite large; you will be downloading multiple software packages over and over again, once for each individual machine.

To schedule Microsoft updates, simply visit the Control Panel and type "updates" in the search bar at the top. The section for the updates utility appears, and once you click on "Windows Update," you have options that include modifying when and how Microsoft update runs on your computer. In addition to setting a time for the computers to get updates, you should also consider scheduling *how* the updates run. Rather than put them on full automatic, you might want to have the updates download but wait for your OK to install or even wait for your OK to download in the first place. The reason I recommend not putting them on full automatic is that, despite all of your scheduling efforts, Windows will occasionally download an update and ignore that schedule entirely. I don't know why; perhaps Microsoft has some hidden ability to notify computers of extremely critical updates and automatically push them to its users.

Either way, the last thing you want is for your users (be they staff or public) to be elbows deep in their latest critical project and suddenly get a pop-up that says, "Your computer will automatically restart in 10 minutes to finish installing updates." I think everyone has had that happen to them at some point, and I, for one, hate it. It never fails to come at the most inopportune time.

Some forms of security software allow you to take control of Microsoft updates in another way. On the client computers, for example, you could turn Microsoft updates to off, and then the third-party security software would take care of instructing each computer as to when, specifically, they should run Microsoft updates. This is described in more detail later in the chapter.

Microsoft updates are perhaps *the most important* type of update that you can run on your computers. It seems like every week we hear about a new security vulnerability in the Windows operating system or other Microsoft products. It's tempting to blame Microsoft and just say, "They make a crummy program with a million security holes," but in reality the blame is shared with malicious developers all over the world, who work far harder at cracking security holes in Microsoft Windows than in any other operating system. This is due to the large market share that Microsoft Windows still maintains. The hackers know that they simply have to find a security hole in Windows and then build a bot or bot net (zombie computers that do whatever the hacker asks) to exploit the security hole automatically on computers all over the world. The reasons that hackers do this vary greatly, but the general point here is that a current patched Microsoft Windows system is much less likely to be vulnerable to these kinds of attacks. That helps you avoid the terrible day when you come to work and discover a security breach or virus has propagated through the network and affected all of your unpatched machines.

Antivirus Updates

Antivirus and antimalware updates are generally controlled through a separate, stand-alone antivirus program on each machine. For example, if you have Symantec Endpoint Protection, each Symantec client program has a "live update" feature that triggers either automatically or when you schedule it. Again, at first these programs are generally set to full automatic update, but you might want to consider scheduling the updates for a particular low-use time if you find bandwidth is becoming an issue for your library. Antivirus updates are generally less likely to request a reboot of your machine than Microsoft updates. The other thing you should schedule through the antivirus program is a regular system scan. Again, schedule this for a low- or no-use time, as they generally pop up a small window, letting you know the progress of the scan when it runs, and also can slow down older machines while the scan is running. You don't necessarily want to have this interrupt someone's work, especially on a public computer, where the user is likely to just hit the "cancel scan" button. If you don't schedule a regular scan, eventually you'll start getting nagging reminders telling you to do so.

Free antivirus options are available. Microsoft makes its own antivirus called Microsoft Security Essentials (or Windows Defender if you're running Windows 8). Whether this can be used in a public library setting is something of a legal gray area. It may be worth getting a lawyer's opinion if you decide to go this route with all of the machines in your building.

Pay-per-license enterprise software, such as Symantec Endpoint Protection, will also sometimes come with software that allows you to control all of your antivirus client programs from a central server. In the Symantec example, the Symantec Endpoint Protection Manager can create custom installations of clients based on parameters you specify and download updates so they are available locally on your network. This means that instead of every client software having to hog the limited Internet bandwidth to download updates individually the clients can download them from the local building server over the much faster internal network.

One other item to be on the lookout for is *major* updates to your particular antivirus software. Sometimes, an update to antivirus software is so complex that it can't be applied through an automatic update process (for example, the difference between Symantec Endpoint Protection version 11 and SEP 12.1). These upgrades will therefore have to be installed manually on each machine.

Third-Party Updates

Third-party updates are where things really start to get sticky and where it would be a strong advantage to create a grid or some form of a schedule to keep track of which updates need to be run and when. It is an unfortunate truth that some programs have automatic updating features and some do not. Some allow you to schedule when the updates occur and some do not. You need to consider this when determining how to create your schedule. The following is my list of mandatory software that needs to be installed and regularly updated:

Java Runtime Environment

www.java.com

When someone says they're installing Java or the web page requires Java, this is what they mean. The Java website will automatically select the correct version for you to download and install. From there, you simply set updates to fully automatic or scheduled or fully manual. Java has a notorious nag screen and pop-ups that remind you *constantly* to update Java if you haven't done so. Despite the numerous worries in the news about the security of Java over the years, many web pages, including major ones like the National Weather Service and the United States Army, still require Java on some of their pages as of this writing.

Adobe Reader

http://get.adobe.com/reader

The free Adobe Reader software is still the industry standard for opening PDF files, although in Windows 8 the default is a Microsoft PDF reader app that generally does the job. Still, it is in your best interest to have this installed and available on all of your machines. These updates are always automatically downloaded; they cannot be scheduled. Adobe Reader will pop a notification in the system tray telling you when a new update is ready to be installed. There is a free alternative to Adobe Reader called Foxit Reader (www.foxitsoftware.com/downloads/), which is gaining traction quickly. The Foxit Reader website claims it has over 275 million users; I have used Foxit personally and it works well. The only major issue with Foxit is that people are sometimes confused with functions and button arrangement in Foxit because they are used to the layout of Adobe Reader. Either program would perform fine. Foxit has its own updater that isn't covered here.

Adobe Flash Player

http://get.adobe.com/flashplayer

This program is, finally, beginning to make its exit. For many years, Adobe Flash Player was the industry standard for publishing motion content on the web. What started with pre-programmed Flash "animations" developed over the years to become no less than the base platform for delivering video content on YouTube. However, in just the past couple of years, the introduction of HTML5 has changed the way that web content is delivered. HTML5 is, as the name suggests, a new version of the language that essentially defines how web pages are laid out and seen all over the world. HTML5 rolls into the core web browsing capabilities some functions that used to require separate plug-ins; one of these is full-motion streaming video (FMV). Because FMV is now a core component of the latest versions of web pages and browsers, in the near future Adobe Flash Player will no longer be needed on new machines. Currently, the functionality of Adobe Flash Player is integrated into the Internet Explorer browser, but only on Windows 8 and above. Therefore, if you are running Windows 8 or above, it is not necessary to download Adobe Flash Player separately. However, if you have any machines running Windows 7 or under, you will need to download and install the Adobe Flash Player plug-in in order for the user to have a full-content experience on the current Internet. The plug-in gives you an option while it is being installed to update automatically from that point forward. If you choose this, be aware that you cannot reverse your choice without uninstalling the program. Further, you cannot schedule the updates; they happen when the updates are ready. Fortunately, Adobe Flash Player is a fairly small download, and the updates are generally even smaller than the core plug-in.

Computer Driver Updates

Websites vary depending on computer make.

Drivers are special bits of software that allow your computer operating system to communicate with the hardware components attached to the computer. For example, the computer cannot communicate correctly with a printer attached to it without some sort of driver software. Most likely drivers (even if they are generic ones provided by Windows) are already installed for all the hardware components on your computer from the Network Interface Card to the keyboard. Occasionally, a driver might not be installed, and Windows will have no generic option. In this case, you'll have to go to the hardware manufacturer's website and follow the directions there to download an appropriate driver.

The IT world has varying opinions about driver updates. One camp says that you should schedule a trip to the manufacturer's website every month, just to check and make sure there are no new drivers for your machine. If there are new drivers, install them immediately for the best performance. It is correct to say that drivers sometimes improve hardware performance.

The other camp says, "If it works, why try to break it?" This group says that sometimes the latest drivers, even if they are technically correct for your hardware, can actually cause the hardware to stop working or cause a reduction in performance. It is also correct to say that sometimes a driver update is the wrong choice for your machine, even when it is endorsed by the manufacturer.

So where do we meet in the middle on this? Personally, as the only IT professional on staff, you should fall into the second category, which is: "Don't touch or tinker with what works." Instead, visit the manufacturer's website and read the **release notes** for the latest version of the driver. The release notes are written to tell you *before you install the driver* what kind of updates the driver provides for your hardware. Is it a performance update? Does it correct a critical security loophole? Or does it just update the manufacturer's logo to the latest version (no kidding!). I generally only install drivers when there is a critical security fix or a serious degradation in performance of the hardware or if I know for certain that the hardware is malfunctioning with the current driver.

In addition to the individual manufacturer's websites, drivers are generally available from the support website of your particular computer vendor (such as Toshiba or Dell). Some sites such as Dell even allow you to put in a service tag number for your particular computer and the correct drivers will be automatically selected for that specific machine based on the manufacturer's records of the hardware when it left the factory. Modern drivers download just like any other executable program, and you simply double-click on the installation file to begin. Once the installation is complete, you may be asked to reboot the computer, at which point the operating system will re-detect the hardware and apply the new drivers automatically.

When and if you install updated drivers is your choice. Some computers come pre-installed with "system check" software that contacts the manufacturer's website and offers to apply the latest drivers to your machine automatically. Opinions vary on this as well, but I would strongly recommend that you disable or even uninstall any of these programs. The last thing you want is for a public user or staff member to be firing off their own driver updates and messing up the computer so badly that you have no choice but to wipe and start from scratch. Knowing how to fix a computer when you've screwed it up yourself is one thing. Knowing how to fix a computer when you have no idea how it got screwed up and the person who screwed it up walked out the door 20 minutes ago, that's something else again.

BIOS Updates

The final type of third-party update is a BIOS update, also known as a firmware update. Essentially, **BIOS**, which is short for **Basic Input Output System**, is the lowest-level program that tells your computer how to be a computer and communicate with other hardware. Its strongest effects are felt before the operating system loads—at that point BIOS has complete control. However, BIOS affects the performance of a computer even after you are in Windows. Everything from the power save and sleep functions to the processor fan speed can trace itself back to control in the BIOS program.

BIOS updates, more than any other update, can change the very functioning of your machine. BIOS updates act like "revisions" of your particular computer model, in much the same way that some popular Windows software undergoes revisions. These changes will often improve performance and perhaps even unlock new features of computer hardware. Sometimes they can provide a correction to a major problem with the machine, such as a laptop with exceptionally high fan speed based on incorrect internal temperature reporting.

However, updating the BIOS is a serious matter. When you run the BIOS update program, your computer reboots, essentially erases core programming, and rewrites it with a new version. Years ago, when modern programs did not help you do this automatically, updating the BIOS was a very tricky and often messy process. There were few or no safety checks (you had to *know for certain* that you had the correct BIOS version and that the update was complete and uncorrupted) and you could willy-nilly write any BIOS programming over your own. If the programming was incorrect, it would effectively ruin your computer, called **bricking**. Bricking is a friendly term to describe what your computer becomes if you screw up a BIOS update—it turns into a brick. If you mess up the BIOS, all the computer is good for is building material; the computer is permanently unable to boot. There are a very few manufacturers (more all the time) that offer an extremely convoluted method for "unbricking" your computer, but you shouldn't rely on this being available.

Fortunately, many modern-day BIOS update utilities are much safer for the following reasons:

1. They can be started from within Windows, preventing mistakes at the command prompt.
2. They automatically perform a checksum routine to make sure the new BIOS file is completely accurate and does not contain errors.

3. They detect the BIOS make and model and can generally prevent you from applying a firmware update that is not appropriate for your machine.
4. They can prevent you from updating the firmware of a laptop without it being plugged into a wall outlet.

All this adds up to the fact that manufacturers have basically idiot-proofed updating the BIOS on your machines, and it is now only slightly more difficult than a regular driver update. *One thing of which you must be aware is that any loss of power during the BIOS update process will brick your computer.* Don't do the update during a thunderstorm or during a time when building power may be unstable, and don't do it on a laptop unless the laptop is plugged in to a wall outlet.

Here is a quick primer on how a typical BIOS update works, using the Dell support website as an example:

1. Type in the service tag of your computer and the website draws together driver updates for your specific computer.
2. Click on the BIOS section and download the latest recommended BIOS by date. This is usually a regular executable (.exe) program.
3. Run the program *with administrator privileges* (right-click and click "Run as Administrator").
4. The program displays the current version of the BIOS and the version to which you will be updating. If all the integrity checks are passed, the utility gives you an option to proceed.
5. If you have an administrator or "setup" password for your BIOS/CMOS setup screens, you may be asked to enter it at this point.
6. Confirm that you want to apply the update, and the computer reboots and the BIOS update process begins. The computer will appear to stop completely right after it reboots, and a special set of screens will appear, informing you of the progress of the BIOS update. Your computer speaker may also chirp as an indication of the progress.
7. The computer may reboot once or twice more. Let it do everything automatically, and **do not under any circumstances** touch the power switch or unplug the computer. When the process is complete you will be sent back into Windows.

That's really all there is to it. If it gets more complicated than that, you need to consider either not doing the BIOS update (which is okay unless your computer is malfunctioning somehow and you truly need it) or contacting a professional with more experience to complete the update. There are "readme.txt" text files generally available on the support website or in the installer package that will walk you through the steps for more complicated updates, if you decide to try to figure it out yourself.

MAINTENANCE ROUTINES

In addition to updates, there are specific system utilities integrated into the Microsoft Windows operating system that should be run on a regular basis. Two of these, Disk Defragmenter and Disk Cleanup, are discussed here. Please note that there are many free alternative defragmentation and cleanup programs online, from the reliable to the unreliable. Those won't be covered in this book simply because there are an untold number available. Once you understand the purpose of Disk Defragmentation and Disk Cleanup, you will be able to make an informed decision about whether to continue using the Microsoft Windows system utilities or find alternatives on your own.

Temporary files are files used by programs on a temporary basis. When a program needs to temporarily store data, it creates files on the computer hard drive and parks the data in those files. Programs are supposed to clean up after themselves and delete temporary files, but often do not for various reasons. Some programs have persistent temporary files (such as Internet Explorer) that are intended to create a faster Internet experience by making commonly used files readily available from the hard drive rather than having to download the files each time.

Disk Cleanup is a tool that allows you to clear off temporary files from your computer. Clearing off temporary files frees up space on the computer hard drive and can increase computer performance. This utility should be run *before* the Disk Defragmentation utility; see later in this chapter for more on defragmentation. To run Disk Cleanup, simply press ⊞ + R on your keyboard, and from the Run dialog box, type "cleanmgr" and press Enter.

Select the drive that you want to clean up from the window that appears and wait while the computer calculates how much space is available to clean up. The main Disk Cleanup window will show the total amount of space that can be cleaned up and suggest various categories of files to delete. These can be selected or de-selected, depending upon your preference. If you aren't sure, start with the default selections or click on a category to see a description of it. When you're ready to proceed, simply click "Clean up system files." Close the window when the process is finished.

Defragmentation is the process of putting the various pieces of files on your hard drive next to one another so that they are more quickly available when needed from the hard drive. When a file is saved to the hard drive, the file is generally split into parts. The data in these parts is saved to the first available location on the hard drive in order to speed up the saving process. However, this may mean that various pieces of files are in physically distant locations on the drive, which increases the amount of time needed to load the file. Defragmentation reverses this process by rearranging file parts so they are as physically close to one another as possible on the drive, which decreases the amount of time needed to load a file.

Disk Defragmenter is a defragmentation utility that simply rearranges the files and parts of files on your computer to more efficient locations on the hard drive. Disk Defragmenter can be located by pressing ⊞ + R on your keyboard, typing "dfrgui" in the Run dialog box, and pressing Enter. Then you are presented with a window that allows you to select which drive you wish to defragment (generally you will only have one) and two buttons: "Analyze disk" and "Defragment disk." There is really no point to analyzing the disk to see if it needs to be defragmented; just do the defragment on a regular basis, about once a month, and it won't take very long to complete. The utility can detect when files are already physically next to each other and doesn't waste time trying to rearrange those. Once the defragmentation is complete, simply close the window. While you can work while Disk Defragmenter is running, it does sometimes slow the computer down. It might be best to run it overnight or at times of low usage.

PROTECTING YOUR PUBLIC MACHINES FROM ABUSE

Now that we've gone through the types of updates that are required for your machines and looked at some maintenance routines, it's time to look at another facet of security for your public computers, one which can save you many hours of work and headaches by preventing unwanted changes to your machines.

Persistent State Software

Persistent state software is a special type of software that allows you to "freeze" your computer in a specific configuration. You can set up your computer in a specific way—for example, with all of the icons in their correct positions, the updates applied, the Internet favorites in place, and the programs all ready to go for a public user. Then using a configuration utility, you "lock" the persistent state software. After the software is locked, the patron or patrons are free to use the computer. When the computer is rebooted, *everything goes back to exactly the way it was when you set it up*. All of the user's changes and personal information on that computer are erased entirely. In fact, this type of software works so well that even if a patron downloads malicious software or a virus, a simple reboot with the computer in locked mode will often erase all traces of the malicious software.

In the early days, products such as Centurion Technology's Cornerstone (www.centuriontech.com) were partially hardware based. If any librarians or patrons out there remember the original Bill and Melinda Gates Grant computers, then you no doubt remember the large physical hardware lock on the front of the machine that turned the persistent state on or off for each computer.

Today, these products are entirely software based. How they work is incredibly complicated in detail, but the theory behind them is actually quite simple. When a machine is in the "locked" state, the software redirects all data written to the hard drive to a temporary location, away from the original files on the drive. The original files are not modified in any way. Once the computer is rebooted, the temporary data written to the hard drive is erased, and the next user is left with a pristine set of original files. Because user changes are wiped out, this software is obviously not appropriate for computers where user changes are intended to be permanent (such as staff computers!). However, for general-use public computers, patrons often appreciate knowing that their personal data won't inadvertently get left behind.

Sounds like a great deal, right? Here's the rub: Administrative changes, such as the updates listed earlier in this chapter, have to be done with the persistent state software *disabled* or else the updates you just applied (or that the computer applied automatically) won't stick at all and will be erased at the next reboot, like all other user changes.

For instance, let's say you have a public computer with Microsoft updates set to full automatic. New updates are available, so your machine downloads and installs them, as it has been told. Then the patron leaves and the computer reboots. The temporary files, including the updates that were "installed," are wiped out. The updates were not permanently installed, and Windows again sees that new updates are available to download, so it downloads them *again*. And then they are erased again and so on and so forth. Multiply this by several machines in the building and you'll notice not only a reduction in processing speed on the computers but also that a huge chunk, if not all, of your bandwidth is being eaten up by these updates.

This same scenario applies to any software that has an automatic updating program or runs features automatically (such as scheduled antivirus scans).

Making scheduled updates work in your library with persistent state software has two major components:

1. If possible, schedule updates to run at a particular time and day. It won't be perfect, but you can have the machines unlocked so that when the updates do want to run they can run once and be done with it.
2. If your persistent state network control software (discussed later) allows you an option to force Microsoft updates to run on client machines, you may want to disable Microsoft updates entirely and then simply use the "force" option when you are ready to apply Microsoft updates (typically about once a week).

Most software comes with some sort of a scheduling option. Some (such as Adobe Flash Player) you may have to set to full manual updating and run by hand at each machine, because the only other option presented is full automatic with no scheduling, and that doesn't really play well with persistent state software.

The other component of persistent state software that will help with some of these issues is network control software. Generally, the company that manufactures the persistent state software also produces network control software that can be run on a server. This software detects all of the persistent state client programs running on your machines and allows you to be able to control them all from one location and at one time. Compare this with having to physically go to each machine if, for example, you want to unlock all of them so they can wait for scheduled updates. Often this network control software also has its own scheduling feature so that the commands it issues can run automatically at a specified time. However, I tend to issue the commands by hand so that I can have more control over when exactly they run.

Once you schedule updates to run on the client machines with this scenario, the only catch is that *you have to make sure that the machines are unlocked at the correct time and day*. If you don't, the automatic updates will proceed anyway according to schedule and you'll have the same mess of constantly repeating updates until you do unlock them. Make sure you either have the unlock process auto-scheduled through the network control software or have someone else trained to do the job in case you happen to be out sick that day.

While we're on the topic, you should always make sure that the persistent state software is locked and protected whenever you are not actively performing updates. This ensures that personal information on a computer is not accidentally captured and retained. In one scenario, you might unlock a computer to run updates and then forget that the computer is unlocked. A patron comes along, accesses his email on the machine, and then forgets to log out of his e-mail, simply closing the browser and leaving the computer. You then come back to the machine later, unaware that the previous patron didn't log out of his Hotmail account and lock the machine. From that point forward, no matter how many times the machine is rebooted, any patron trying to pull up Hotmail on that machine will be dropped into our example patron's account, all because the original patron forgot to log out and then you made that change persistent!

The fix is easy, however. Simply unlock the computer again and clear your Internet cache (temporary files and history in each installed browser). That should resolve the problem.

There are a couple of ways to prevent the scenario I just described. First, if you are going hands-on with each computer, make sure you don't bite off more than you can chew. In other words, instead of unlocking 10 computers and trying to work on them all at once, unlock one or two computers at a time, put up out of order signs, and keep them monitored till you are finished with updates.

Second, don't leave updates running unattended if possible. If it is a huge update (which they sometimes are), you can unprotect the computer and then log in as an administrator. Once you log in as an administrator, you can start the updates, then press ⊞ + L to lock the administrator account on the computer. Since the patrons won't know the administrator password, the computer is safe, with updates running in the background, until you return to service it.

If you aren't going hands-on with every computer in the building and just want to do regularly scheduled automatic updates on every machine at once, many persistent state network control programs have an option that allow you to disable the keyboard and mouse on a machine automatically whenever the machine's persistent state software is unlocked. The upside is that the patrons can't mess with the machine while it's updating. The downside is that if you need to regain control of the machine for some reason it can be more difficult to do so.

Persistent state software is an excellent way to maintain quality control over your machines. Be aware, however, that since these programs do have to play some tricks with the hard drive data (as described earlier in this chapter) they can cause increased load times on older machines. Manufacturers of this type of software will adamantly claim that they aren't responsible for any slowdown. However, in my experience only current modern machines completely escape any drag created by these programs. Regardless, the greatly increased security you'll get is worth the minor trade-off of a small decrease in response times.

Patron Authentication Software

Another type of program that I think pairs well with persistent state software is **patron authentication software**, such as Envisionware's PC Reservation (http://www .envisionware.com). This software presents a log-in screen on each client computer, and the patron must enter information, usually a library card number, in order to authenticate and gain access to the computer. Often, the computer use policy of the library can be presented as a part of the log-in function of this program.

Once the patron is logged in, the patron authentication software provides the patron with an on-screen timer that tells them how much time they have remaining in the computer session. When the time elapses, the computer is automatically restarted, which is then the persistent state software's cue to restore the computer back to its default state, erasing any personal data from the last user in the process.

The patron authentication software works by contacting a "management" program (basically a small server program), which is installed on a staff-only computer on the same network. This management program is responsible for authenticating patron information provided by the patron at a client machine. Most often, the management program takes a library card number provided at a machine, then turns around and asks the library's **integrated library system (ILS)** whether or not the patron card number is valid and if there are any exceptions to the record. Exceptions are any reason that a patron should not be allowed to use a computer, such as excessive fines or an intentional block placed on the account by a staff member.

If everything with the account checks out, the patron is provided a certain session time based on a wide variety of configurable rules. If the card number is invalid or the patron has an exception, they are denied access to the computer and asked to visit the front desk.

Some forms of patron authentication software also allow patrons to make reservations with a library card to ensure that a computer is available for the patron at a point in the future. Often, patron authentication software is a part of a suite of programs that can allow patrons to pay for print jobs, resolve fines, and complete a host of other tasks.

However, even with just the basic patron authentication software, the program should do three things:

1. Check to make sure the patron is allowed to use the computer.
2. Time the patron's session so the patron can't monopolize a computer for the whole day.
3. Reboot the computer at the end of sessions so that persistent state software can kick in and wipe personal data from the machine.

Patron authentication software licenses are not especially cheap, and the start-up cost may be even greater than the yearly "maintenance" payments thereafter. However, I strongly recommend having this software in your library, especially if you're still using the old, "sign into the computer log book at the front desk" system. Many states have patron confidentiality laws, and the general public being able to walk up and see which patrons are using computers and when may be a violation of those laws.

It should be noted that one final benefit of the patron authentication software is that the management program will keep statistics on how often the library computers are being used and for how long. This is extremely helpful not only from a "library annual report" perspective but also from an IT perspective. If you analyze statistics over the course of a month and find that one computer in particular has usage that's dropped like a rock, it's probably time to evaluate that computer and make sure that there isn't an issue that is keeping patrons away from that machine. Conversely, if you see exceptionally high usage in one lab or area, it may be time to consider getting more machines for that area.

A combination of computer updates, security software, and authentication software will ensure that your computers, both public and staff, continue to run at peak performance. Though security and authentication software is not cheap, the reduced time spent on computer issues makes these types of programs well worth the cost.

CHAPTER 12

Procurement

At some point, simply because you're the only one who knows what's going on as far as technology is concerned, you'll probably be responsible for the library budget line items that involve technology. Think of them as "sub-budgets" of the main budget. You may be the director of your own organization, but even if you're not, don't be surprised if you're granted a large amount of control over this part of the budget once you've gained the confidence of your supervisor. Even if the supervisor is responsible for ordering office supplies and other necessities for day-to-day operations, the ordering of computers and other electronics may fall to you as the IT person.

The prep-work of the procurement process is to have completed some of the other steps in this book ahead of time, namely to triage your major problems and then inventory your machines once those problems are under control.

The first step in the actual procurement process is to obtain a "number," a total figure of what you are allowed to spend for a particular time period. Ideally, you'd get one number, say $5,000, which you are allowed to spend over the course of a fiscal year any way you'd like. In this scenario, you use a simple Excel spreadsheet and create a worksheet with a formula that sums all of the line items. Simply enter the line items and you'll automatically see the total at the end, which tells you how close you are to reaching your budget goal or how far you've gone over.

Start by creating two empty columns, one for item descriptions and one for item costs. Go ahead and create the formula to total the blank "item costs" column. Now, as you determine which purchasing needs should be addressed this year, simply insert a row each time you think of a new item. We're about to fill in the blanks for the item costs. The spreadsheet in Table 12.1 shows a slightly more elaborate version.

Table 12.1   A Sample Technology Budget

Qty	Description	Unit Cost	Total Cost
5	Desktop Computers	$800.00	$4,000.00
1	Color Laser Printer	$500.00	$500.00
2	LCD Monitors 22"	$200.00	$400.00
	Grand Total		$4,900.00

For this example, we've been charged with the purchase of five new desktop computers for the public to use. You should become friends with a sales representative in your technology company of choice; this is discussed in greater detail in the next chapter. But the short version is this: The very first thing you do is pick up the phone and call the sales representative. Explain your project, discuss your system requirements and his or her recommendations, and ask for information on any sales or promotions that are going on within the company. Don't be afraid to explain your situation and explain how tight your budget is; just like car salespersons, in the end they'll sell you a $15,000 car over a $30,000 car rather than have you walk out of the showroom with no sale at all.

At the end of your discussions, the salesperson should provide you with a formal quote, *in writing*, of the price he or she is extending to you for these computers (a document attached to e-mail counts as in writing). A quote can be formal, but it is also merely a statement of possibility; it puts you under no obligation to purchase the product. The quote then allows you to shop around, comparing prices from various companies. Upon receiving a quote, you also have the option to sit on it for a couple of days and then return to the salesperson and say that, after consideration, the extended price isn't good enough. Sometimes they can do even better.

Once you have a couple of quotes from different companies, go ahead and pick the lowest and stick that into your budgeting chart. Repeat this process for each line item.

That's the short version of filling out your technology budget for the year. Get quotes from at least two manufacturers for each line item to make sure that you are getting the best deal for your library.

STAYING WITHIN THE LINES—AND WITHIN THE LAW

When you're collecting these quotes for technology purchases, you need to be intimately familiar with any policies that your organization has regarding purchasing. For example, in a typical municipality, purchases under $500 may only need one quote (though you should get at least two more just to be sure). However, for purchases *over* $500, you may be *required* to obtain at least three formal quotes, keep documentation, and perhaps even file them with your supervisor or with the city accounting department. And it gets *more* complicated: Past a certain purchase price ($5,000 in our example), you may be *required* to publish a formal **Request for Proposals (RFP)** or **Request for Bids (RFB)**.

RFPs and RFBs are formally written, publicly available documents that outline to vendors the specific criteria of what you are trying to purchase. For example, say you are purchasing 10 computers. You would outline the system requirements for the machines, stopping short of specifying a particular make or model of system. Then it would be up to each vendor to match their company's products to your criteria and submit a formal response to the RFP or RFB that outlines what they will provide and at what cost, as well as any other terms and conditions that apply. Generally, the difference between an RFP and an RFB is that an RFP is a request for services (such as redesigning your website), while an RFB is a request for goods, such as a bid for desktop computers. However, use of the terminology can vary widely. Check with your organization's policies or finance officer to make sure you are using the correct terminology.

Always follow your organizational policies. Generally, you are required to publish an RFP or RFB, such as in the local newspaper or on your website. You are under no further obligation, however, to chase down vendors who don't respond to the publication, unless you want a quote from their particular company for some reason. Publishing the RFP or RFB ensures that when a competing company catches wind of the opportunity they missed and contacts you about it, you can simply say, "It was published according to policy/law, here and here, on this date."

While there is no single correct way to write an RFP or RFB, your city or other organization may have a standard form or format that they want you to use. Policies may be in place for agencies writing proposals so that you may be required to ask your supervisor before choosing a foundation for a funding proposal. Barring any guidance from your supervisor, see if you can obtain an old RFP or RFB that was successfully used and simply modify the wording and formatting of that one to fit your needs. Many books and articles have been written describing how to write proposals, and you could borrow these from your state library.

The RFP or RFB doesn't necessarily have to be a long or complicated document. When it comes to specifying individual technological items for bid, make sure you are as specific as possible while at the same time word your document such that your requirements are the bare minimum that are required. For example:

Waldorf Public Library is seeking bids for the purchase of five desktop computers. Minimum system requirements for these machines are as follows:

- Intel i5 processor or equivalent or greater
- 4.0 GB RAM or greater
- 500 GB hard disk drive or greater
- 3-year NBD on-site warranty

The words "minimum system requirements" and "or greater" mean that your requirements are only a starting point. That opens you up in case a vendor can cut you a competitive deal on machines that are even better than the specs you initially requested. This *does* happen, especially with major companies such as Dell that sometimes have to make a tiered range of models fit your proposal requirements. Rather than select the computer that doesn't quite meet the requirements, they select the one that's at the "next tier up," which is sometimes higher than the specs you requested.

Also, note the words "for the purchase of." This means you aren't interested in leasing the equipment, which is common with photocopiers and is getting more and more common with desktop machines as well.

If you aren't sure what the specifications should be for your computers, don't worry. Just contact a friendly sales representative from one of the vendors, tell them what you're trying to do, and ask them to recommend a machine. Have them send the specifications of the machine to you, then modify the basic system specifications of that machine into the system requirements for your bid process. Again, remember that the vendor probably won't try to sell you on a machine that they don't think will fit your needs, because you won't be happy with it and won't buy again. So have confidence that the basic specification should be somewhat near what you need to bid in your document.

Always, always include a warranty specification. You don't have to know that a particular company's warranty is called the "Gold Super-de-duper level" warranty; again, it's the responsibility of the vendor to determine which of their products best fits your needs. Just specify what you want in a warranty (NBD means next business day repairs) and take it from there.

Next, you'll want to specify the format of the response, if you feel that is necessary. Generally, unless you expect the responses to be 20 pages long (as with a website redesign), you won't need to specify formatting that the responding vendors must use. However, it is helpful to insist that vendors have a line-by-line breakdown of the purchase cost if you are bidding for multiple items. It does happen every now and then that you'll get a response similar to the following:

Mom and Pop Computer Shop
Dear Sir,
In response to your Request for Bid we are pleased to submit the following bid:
Desktop computers A20344 Qty.10 $9,600.00
Thank you for allowing us the opportunity to bid!

While this is technically a "response," it doesn't really tell you anything about the specifications of the systems that they're offering, and it doesn't allow you to check to make sure that those systems actually meet your minimum system requirements as specified in the RFB or RFP. Make sure you explain that you'll need the technical details outlined in each response. If someone still submits a bid like the one given earlier, it's up to you whether you want to go back and allow them to re-bid or simply reject the bid outright (following your organization's policies, of course).

If you do write your own RFP or RFB, be sure to include at least one line that mentions four things:

1. You (the library) have the right to reject any proposal for any reason.
2. You are under no obligation to accept any of the proposals.
3. The vendors are responsible for obtaining clarification from you if they feel the RFP or RFB is not clear.
4. You are under no obligation to go with the lowest bid if it is not qualified.

Be especially careful with No 4; try to find wording that has been used successfully or consult your supervisor or counsel such as the city attorney. One time, three separate computer shops bid on a project that included purchasing desktop computers and flatbed scanners. One computer shop in particular bid way, way below the other vendors. However, in reading the fine print of the response, it was clear that the shop had misread the RFB intentionally or unintentionally. The scanner quoted did not even come close to meeting the requirements specified in the proposal; it was the wrong size, did not have the proper resolution, etc. In that instance, we documented the anomaly, kept it on file, and selected the next lowest bid, which met all of the criteria.

Finally, make sure you specify a deadline for returning responses, as well as how and where the responses should be delivered. Most times, e-mail responses will suffice, although for larger projects you may even want to insist on mailed bids (so you can verify the date they were sent for qualification purposes) or even require sealed bids. **Sealed bids** are bids that are not opened until a specified time and day to protect confidentiality of the submitting vendors and to insure the general integrity of the bids. While sealed bids may be received on various times and days, they must be kept in a secure location (preferably under lock and key) until the date and time of the bid opening. If you are thinking about requiring sealed bids, it would be best to consult your supervisor and legal counsel to make sure that you are staying within the law. Especially with bids over $10,000, things can get ugly in a hurry if one of the bidding vendors thinks that the process wasn't on the up-and-up. Don't give them any reason to question your methods.

Always, always, always, always document EVERYTHING. Make a folder and put all of your documents for a particular purchasing process inside and keep that folder for as long as your organization's policies require. As an example, you can return to the documentation when the "low" bidder blows the scanner requirements and the vendor calls back and asks why the bid was not selected. You can go right to your documentation and tell them exactly where their bid did not meet the criteria.

Also, check your organization's policy on clarifying an RFP or RFB after it's been published. If a particular vendor calls you up and says, "This point on your RFB is ambiguous or confusing" and then you clarify that point for them, you may be required to either publish that clarification in writing the same way that the initial RFP/RFB was published *or* provide "equal opportunity" by contacting all respondents with that clarification and offering them the opportunity to revise their response.

The RFP or RFB will normally have a specific deadline by which companies must respond in order to be considered in the process. Once that date has passed, start by creating a **mail-merge database** so that you can provide mail responses to all of the applicants, both successful and unsuccessful. Once the database is created, Microsoft Word has special mail-merge features that allow it to "read" the records one at a time from the database and put that information on an envelope or another document. So once the database is created, you can run a mail-merge job in Microsoft Word and avoid having to type 20 separate envelopes by hand; Word will create and print each one automatically. If you only have three responses, mail-merge may be overkill, but sometimes you receive a lot more and it can be a blessing. Directions for creating a mail-merge database are available online.

A **mail-merge database** is a database file generally constructed in Microsoft Access, which contains the names and contact information of all of the bidding entities.

After creating the database, collect all of the response documents and carefully sort them by which ones meet the requirements as outlined in your request and which ones do not. Once, while working with an RFP for the redesign of our library website, we received 32 responses, of which a solid one-quarter of them did not meet the minimum criteria outlined in our request for proposals and were immediately disqualified. Another four were included in our pool but were out of serious consideration immediately; we expected to spend (and eventually did) about $20,000 for the website, and these four vendors each submitted a bid in excess of $100,000.

Again, *keep everything*. Even if a vendor is grossly inadequate for some reason and disqualified immediately, keep all of the documents on file for as long as your organization requires. In your mail-merge database, create a field to mark which vendors were rejected and which one you end up accepting.

Once you have it narrowed down to the vendors that appear to qualify, find the lowest bidder in the stack. *Carefully* check that document again against your specific requirements as outlined in your RFB and make sure that the vendor has met all of them. If the vendor has met your requirements and is a reasonable bid that is near what you expected to spend, then you have a winner. However, if you find the low bid fails to meet requirements, shift it to the discard stack and move to the next lowest bidder until you have one that is successful.

CONTACT AFTER THE PROCESS

Unless your public records laws or policies require it, you are under no obligation to reveal to competing vendors what dollar amounts other companies bid or what individual proposals looked like. In fact, many times the proposals themselves are stamped confidential material by the vendor, although public records laws such as Missouri's Sunshine Law would likely override these considerations if they were ever formally requested by the public to view. However, many vendors will still ask for this information on the off chance that you might give it to them. From an ethical standpoint, don't, unless you are required to do so.

It is, however, good practice to send a letter to every organization that responds to your initial request. For all but one organization, this letter will state simply that you appreciate the response, but another vendor was selected. It is okay to name the winning vendor in this letter and the city and state location if the vendor is not local.

Dos and Don'ts When Sending a Response Letter

Don't provide excessive detail about responses, dollar amounts, or other points that could be either unethical or the seed for a formal complaint against your organization.
Do thank the vendors profusely and encourage them to bid on other projects in the future.
Don't promise to put them on a mailing list automatically notifying them of future RFPs or RFBs. That puts you under too much obligation.
Do use formal block style for each letter and sign each letter by hand.

One final note on RFPs and RFBs: If you feel like you are in over your head, then contact someone with more experience to assist you. For example, you would never, ever, ever be expected to write the RFB for a building renovation project. In this case, the engineering and architectural firm that you work with is the one who handles all of that process. The firm has special software that allows them to put together a (generally) legally bulletproof RFB with very little wiggle room, which construction companies can then receive and to which they can respond. A full RFB for a building renovation can contain hundreds of pages and comes in a thick, three-ring binder.

Not to scare you off of the process, but RFPs and RFBs do have some legal implications and could be the basis for a potential lawsuit if not conducted according to applicable organizational policies and laws. If you have your organization's policy available to you when constructing an RFP, you probably won't run into any issues.

PLACING AND RECEIVING YOUR ORDER

We'll assume from this point forward that you have conducted a successful RFP/RFB and you now have your winning vendor. You've also sent out the appropriate letters, and you're ready to order. When you submit the order, make sure you provide all of your library's contact information and your name. Most vendors include a bid or quote number with their response. Make sure to provide the quote number as well as the date the quote was submitted and the name of any sales representative who was responsible for the quote. Submit the order and then within 24 hours follow up by phone or e-mail to make sure the order was received.

Make sure when you place the order that the order is sales tax exempt if your library qualifies for this. Normally, public libraries are sales tax exempt; contact your supervisor to confirm this. You may be required to provide a copy of the official state tax exemption letter to the vendor for them to keep on file.

If possible, while your order is being processed, obtain tracking numbers so you can keep an eye on the status of your shipment(s). This helps you to not only know when to expect the shipment, but also which carrier will be delivering the packages. All of the major carriers have online tools that allow you to check tracking numbers on the fly. If the shipment is quite large, be sure to prepare an area in your library in advance where you will perform the order unpacking and check in when the items arrive. Request that the delivery person physically place the boxes in your staging area, if possible. Generally, the delivery person will work with you on this.

Once the order arrives, carefully inspect the labels to make sure that all of the boxes are present. For example, UPS shipping labels say "Package 1 of 3," letting you know that in the particular shipment, there are two more packages. All of your boxes should arrive at once, unless you've been notified by the carrier or the vendor that some were shipped separately. Immediately inspect the boxes to make sure that there is no visible damage. The boxes probably will be scuffed, but they should not have holes, large crush marks, etc. If ANY package appears to be damaged, tell the driver to wait while you open the package and examine the contents. They might not want to do this, but insist that they stay put until you make sure the articles are not damaged.

If any damage to the contents has occurred, immediately ask the delivery person to note it and/or file a claim with the carrier. Even though most "signatures" are now done electronically, there are procedures in place for noting and initialing damage like you used to do with the old carbon copy shipping documents. Insist that these procedures be followed and ask the driver what the next steps are for resolution. If possible, have the driver provide you with some sort of a paper copy acknowledging the damage. Once the driver has left, immediately contact the vendor and explain the situation to them and that you had the driver note the damage on delivery. The vendor and carrier should work out a resolution from that point forward. Even if the damage to an item is not apparent until the driver is gone and you've opened the box, be sure to contact and complain to the vendor. They will more than likely be able to work out a solution with you.

Assuming none of your items are damaged, print a copy of your order confirmation from the vendor's website and then find the packing slip that is either attached to the outside or included within one of the shipping boxes. Locate the slip **first.** As you unpack the items, check and double-check against both the order confirmation and the packing slip to ensure that each and every item you ordered is present and accounted for. This is the same method that you would use when receiving a shipment of books to be added to the library collection. Again, if there are any discrepancies, contact the vendor.

Once you have the items unpacked, make sure you put an asset tag on each item if that is the procedure for your technology inventory system. Otherwise, check the items off the packing slip to confirm all are there and you have a record of having unpacked them.

Budgeting for a technology purchase is a fairly simple process. Remember to follow your organization's policies and procedures on procurement, especially when it comes to obtaining a certain number of quotes or providing a formal RFP/RFB for vendors. Know your organization's policy and state and local laws and follow them. Also, use a simple, standard procedure when ordering to make sure that you get the right equipment at the right price and receive it in pristine condition.

CHAPTER 13

The Value of Sales Representatives

Once word gets out that you're the new IT guy in town (and it will get out), expect to start getting the occasional phone call from several different types of companies wanting to sell you goods and services.

The first type are the maintenance contract professionals, who want to help you support your systems, by providing on-site or remote assistance with your technology problems. The second type are companies who want to lease equipment to you. Computer leases do exist, and yes, depending on your budget situation you may find a leasing arrangement to be extremely valuable and cost-effective. Leasing is not covered in detail here, but basically you lease computers in the same way you lease cars for a flat or calculated fee, per month or per year. In about three years, just about the time the computers become obsolete, you will get a fresh batch of new computers. The downside, of course, is that if you decide to stop working with a particular leasing company you don't own the computers, and you're stuck without any machines at all unless the leasing company offers you the option to buy them.

The third type of sales call you may get, and by far the most valuable, is from companies such as CDW (or CDW-G if you're on the government side of things, as with public libraries). CDW will offer to set you up with a "dedicated account representative" to handle any and all of your computer and electronics purchasing needs. A point of clarification: While the "dedicated" account representatives are certainly dedicated to their jobs, you aren't the only client they're serving. Generally, however, clients of a particular sales representative are all either from a certain region of the country or a certain type of industry such as public schools. So expect that while your representative may know something about the industry you're working in, also expect that you'll have to refresh their memory on your particular situation and needs sometimes.

Once you're assigned a dedicated account representative, they'll no doubt make contact with you. If not, you should make an initial contact with them. Why on earth would you want to cold-call a sales representative? Sales representatives have the inside track on the equipment that is going to be right for your organization. In this book, for example, I make a recommendation that you should have a network switch rather than a hub. Fine, so you decide to upgrade to a switch. Here's a short list of questions you're now faced with:

1. Which brand should I get? Which ones are good?
2. Are there differences in switch speeds?
3. How many ports should be on the switch?
4. Managed or unmanaged?
5. VLAN capable or not? What does VLAN even mean?
6. How much power does it draw?
7. How noisy is it? Does that matter?
8. What kind of a warranty does it have?

You can quickly see that a sales representative, who has all of that information right there at his or her fingertips and knows how to access it, can come in handy. You'll have to set aside the fear that he or she is trying to "over-sell" you on something that you don't need. Unlike car dealers, who can sell you on a much more expensive car that you don't need but which still drives like a car, technology is different. If a representative over-sells you, for example, on a really expensive switch with a ton of features, you may find that the switch is difficult or impossible for you to manage or does not function in the way you want it to because you're struggling to set it up. In other words, if a sales representative grossly over-sells clients on products that they don't need, they're much more likely to hear about it than the car dealer. If you are concerned that your representative is trying to over-sell you, tell them so and explain that you want something that will do what you need it to do without being unnecessarily complicated. If they want to keep the business, they'll listen.

A sales representative has multiple company internal databases they can interact with, which allow them to **drill-down** or make selections from a multitude of options to find the correct model for your needs. For example, they can set your price range, number of ports on a switch, and that the switch should be managed and the database spits out a suggestion as to the correct type of switch for your needs. The key is that the sales representative has experience in answering some of the questions posed earlier. For an example of how this works, visit Newegg (http://www.newegg.com). Newegg is a leading direct seller of computer components to consumers, and along the left-hand side of their website, they have an excellent drill-down tool, also called a **facet tool,** which gives you some idea of what the sales representatives might use. Start by picking a category of item, such as "networking components," then a specific type of item such as "wireless routers." You're then provided with a variety of checkboxes and sliders where you can set price and features until Newegg spits out a few results that match your criteria. The drill-down is an interesting and extremely effective way to cull a few results from a large number of options, and it gives some hint of the future of search engines as it relates to metadata.

Metadata is, as it sounds, a somewhat abstract concept, but can best be described as "information about information." So, for example, all of the printers on Newegg will have metadata that specifically defines the pages per minute speed for each printer model. If this metadata is common across all printers, then the drill-down system should work flawlessly when locating printers that match the pages per minute criteria you specified. Metadata can also be thought of as a somewhat more organized form of "tagging"—that early Web 2.0 concept of bloggers adding keywords to each post to make it easier to find via the search tools. For what it's worth, Twitter hashtags really don't do anything at all within Twitter; they simply help cull down an unfathomably large pool of tweets by adding a bit of metadata. By searching for specific hashtags then, you can limit your Twitter results to tweets on a particular topic.

Sales representatives have the inside track on using their specific systems. Go with a company that has sales representatives that you can call, as opposed to just online chatting or e-mailing. A phone call can sometimes be significantly more productive, especially when you have a lot of questions or need to haggle on the price.

CHAPTER 14

Future Planning and Goal Setting

Okay, it's story time. My mother had a plaque hanging in our kitchen when I was a small child. On the plaque was a picture of a blue-eyed kitten, rolling upside down in a field of daisies and looking wistful as kittens often do. Underneath was the caption: "Set aside some dreaming time."

That's what this chapter is about. Once you have a handle on what's going on (even if there are some pending projects), you should take just a minute to stop and dream about the future for your organization and how IT will fit into that future. What do you want to do with technology in the next two years? The next five? Sometimes your organization will have a required long-range plan and you'll be forced to submit goals anyway. But try to do this dreaming when you aren't required to do so. Some of the best ideas for new and exciting ways of using technology can come when you least expect it.

Personally, it will help to keep a free-flowing document that lets some big ideas on paper. You could have something as simple as a legal-sized piece of yellow legal pad paper tacked to your bulletin board. Across the top of this paper, in big, scrawly Sharpie are written the words, "DREAM BOARD," and underneath you put all your ideas, simple and outrageous, for moving technology forward in your library (Figure 14.1). This is the paper you want to keep with all of your ideas, no matter how crazy they may be or how outlandish they may seem. No idea should be discarded. Money is not an object. Time is not an object. Sense is not an object. Set aside some dreaming time.

A second document you should keep (perhaps on computer) is a slightly more formal outline of your needs and goals for the next couple of years. Whereas a goal on the Dream Board could be "get an interactive touch screen directory like you see in a shopping mall!"

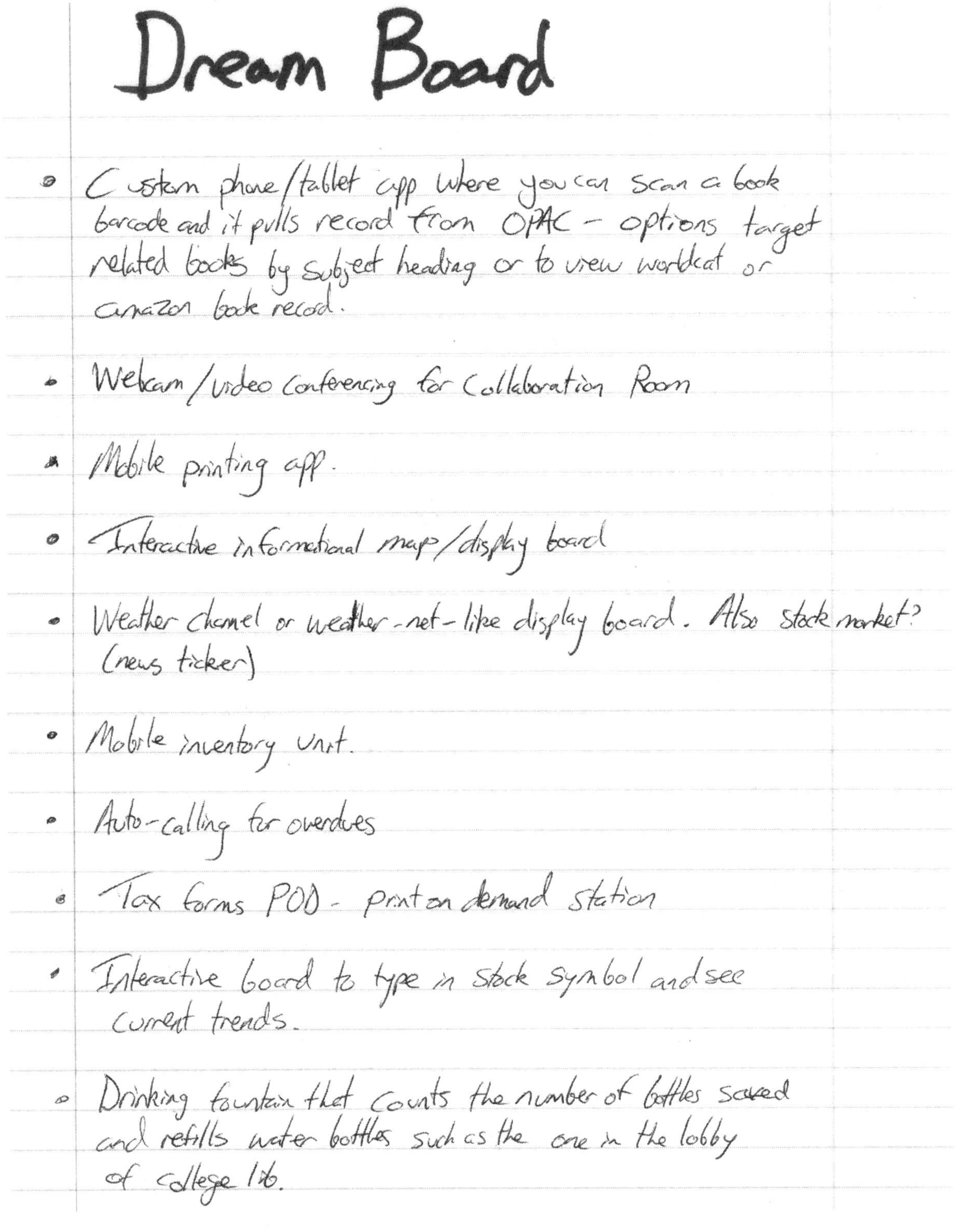

Dream Board

- Custom phone/tablet app where you can scan a book barcode and it pulls record from OPAC – options target related books by subject heading or to view worldcat or amazon book record.

- Webcam/video conferencing for Collaboration Room

- Mobile printing app.

- Interactive informational map/display board

- Weather channel or weather-net-like display board. Also stock market? (news ticker)

- Mobile inventory unit.

- Auto-calling for overdues

- Tax forms POD – print on demand station

- Interactive board to type in stock symbol and see current trends.

- Drinking fountain that counts the number of bottles saved and refills water bottles such as the one in the lobby of college lib.

Figure 14.1 Dream Board

a goal on the more formal document would be "replace three obsolete computers, upgrade two computers to Windows 8."

The formal document is important to have for two reasons:

1. It helps you to make a strong argument during budget time. If your supervisor asks you for input on what needs to be done with technology, you can simply produce this document and help him or her to start funding the next steps to keep the IT side of things running.
2. It is important to have this document in case money suddenly appears from nowhere (as happens occasionally). In a typical scenario, someone dies and ends up being a benefactor to the library. Your supervisor asks you if you have any projects on which you'd like to spend the money, and then you whip out the slightly more formal document and say, "Why, yes, these are the things that need to be done to keep us on track."

In both scenarios, it is much more likely that your projects will be funded and your life will be easier if you have a semi-formal document that keeps track of where you are and where you need to be going in the next couple of years. Formats for these documents vary widely, as well as names for the document. Some are called "Technology Plans," but even those tend to be too formal for what you need unless you are required to keep such a plan for some reason. Our goal is to strike a balance between a document that is easily modifiable and fluid and yet is ready at a moment's notice to be printed out and distributed to whoever may be interested to know what the organization's IT goals are for the future.

So back-tracking for a moment, what's the point of our Dream Board scribble document? Chances are when you first create your Dream Board, you won't be able to do any of the things on the list. They'll all just be ideas, or if they're even remotely feasible, perhaps you can call them long-term goals. However, one day your technology infrastructure will have shifted ever so slightly, and you'll look up at the board and say, "Hey! I can do that now!"

Here's a great example. Our library was struggling with tax season. We were experiencing the following problems:

1. The State of Iowa sent us no (ZERO) printed tax forms, and the federal government only sent a very few.
2. People came into the library looking for, sometimes demanding, paper tax forms.
3. Our staff was willing to help people find tax forms on the public computers to download and print BUT

    a. Staff had limited time.
    b. Many persons needing tax forms did not have the proper credentials for whatever reason to use our public computers (didn't want to or couldn't get a library card, etc.).

The solution, which went on my Dream Board, was to create a kiosk station called a Tax-Forms Print on Demand (POD) station. The station would be a locked-down kiosk that ONLY visited the state and federal tax forms websites. Patrons could quickly sit down, search for, load, and then print the tax forms that they needed.

In the beginning, this wasn't feasible. No spare computer or monitor was available and there was no freely available kiosk software that effectively did what was needed.

A year later, when I looked at the Dream Board, the situation had changed and it was suddenly possible to do it. A spare computer, a spare monitor, and free, open-source software had just been published that would turn any computer into a website kiosk similar to the ones that you see in museums.

When you do something on your Dream Board, you can cross it off. Now it is something that can be listed on your performance evaluation, which shows you are "forward thinking" and "a self-starter."

While there is no right way to do future planning, it is imperative that you have a plan. Whether you find the money or the money finds you, you'll need to know what should be done next at a quick glance. An inventory chart can help enormously in determining specific goals such as "replacing four computers." However, at some level you'll also have to take a global approach and say, "This is the general direction that we want IT to move in this organization." For example, you might currently have several library-owned laptops that are made available to the general public for checkout and use in the library. These laptops may be several years old. Here, you come to a fork in the road. Do you simply replace the laptops with new laptops, or do you replace them with tablets instead? Or do you discontinue the program entirely and divert the funds toward other more used technologies?

Keeping abreast of usage statistics for the devices as well as coming trends in the library profession can help you with this decision. Again, it also helps to get the opinion of your supervisor. Given the trend in libraries as of late, the obvious answer would be tablets, right? Ah, but tablets don't have the same type of persistent-state software, and your desk staff doesn't have time to be "cleaning" the tablets when they come back from each user. On the other hand, users are starting to demand tablets, and they do have the benefit of promoting current technology literacy by teaching patrons how to use "apps," as opposed to programs, and how to navigate and motion with their fingers instead of a mouse.

Again, the decisions you make on your plans are entirely based on the needs of your library. One size DOES NOT fit all, and reject anyone who would tell you that it does. For example, if another professional at another library tells you, "Well, if you don't have tablets for checkout, you're just not keeping up or doing a good job," that's baloney. The other librarian isn't dealing with your budget, isn't in your community, and isn't familiar with your needs. Reject such an argument out of hand.

Goal setting and future planning are imperative to running a tight IT ship in an organization. They help to keep you on track, help you determine "what's next?" as well as help you be prepared during budget time and in the event of an unexpected windfall.

CHAPTER 15

Dealing with the Public 101: Understanding Technology Literacy

Librarians and teachers strive to help students at all levels become information literate. **Information literacy** means an individual is able to quickly recognize the information that they need and is able to effectively and efficiently retrieve that credible information from an appropriate source. It is a concern that so many people Google an answer and never consider it might not be correct. Another concern is the problem that some middle- and high-school teachers see with students citing Wikipedia for research papers; this example goes to the very heart of information literacy. The students are demonstrating that they cannot effectively evaluate information and information sources. They have not yet learned that since Wikipedia can be written and edited by anybody it is probably not a good resource to cite. However, Wikipedia can be a starting point for finding good resources, as well-written articles on Wikipedia often have a "references" section where professional papers and other more reliable information sources are cited as a basis for the Wikipedia article.

Information literacy is inherently tied in with electronic resources. More and more information is available online, and arguably there are fields of study in which, unless the information is obtained immediately through electronic means, it is already obsolete by the time it is published in book form.

Becoming information literate is not necessarily a quick process. It takes some training and some practice to be able to determine a good resource from a poor one. Librarians tend to make it "look easy," because we have done it so often that it really becomes second nature. Teachers and school librarians spend 12 years trying to get their students to be information literate. However, for an average patron in a public library, finding information and evaluating resources can be a time-intensive process.

Because information literacy is so deeply intertwined with computers and the Internet, it is imperative that citizens of a global society have not only information literacy but also technology literacy. **Technology literacy** is the ability to interact with electronic devices in a logical manner that allows the user to quickly learn and manipulate the technology. It allows the user to find common ground to perform essential functions on a device even if they have never seen or used that type of technology before.

Some examples of technology literacy are as follows:

1. Applying what a user knows about their Android phone to make logical guesses that allow them, with some trial and error, to successfully connect an Amazon Kindle Fire to a wireless connection.
2. A user who is able to successfully navigate the Internet in the Opera web browser by applying their experiences with Internet Explorer.
3. A user who is able to navigate in Microsoft Outlook e-mail by applying what they know about navigation in Yahoo! e-mail and in Gmail e-mail.
4. A user who is able to navigate Windows 10 by finding and using the functional similarities brought over from Windows 7.

Opera is a brand name of a web browsing program, just like Internet Explorer and Firefox. Opera is available for free download and use at www.opera.com.

Microsoft Outlook is the flagship e-mail product provided by Microsoft. Previously two separate products, in recent years the Hotmail free e-mail platform has been rolled into a free web version of Outlook.

Yahoo! Mail is the free e-mail product from the Yahoo! search company.

Gmail is the free e-mail service provided by Google, in direct competition with Microsoft and Yahoo. While Outlook and Yahoo organize e-mails in a traditional format by default, Gmail is most noted for organizing e-mail messages into "conversations," such that several e-mail messages sent back and forth between users may show up as a single conversation within the inbox.

Technology literacy is a crisis in the United States. If you've ever worked any sort of a job that requires you to assist John Q. Public with technology, you quickly begin to understand that despite technology taking over a role in nearly every aspect of our modern lives, the ability of the average person to utilize technology has not drastically improved.

Before continuing with the rest of this chapter, it should be acknowledged that the remaining examples are about some mistakes made by library patrons. But the point of this chapter is not to poke fun at or discredit patrons; it is to meet the patron at their current level of technology literacy, whatever that may be, and help them to improve it. This necessitates providing examples of where patrons were unable to perform simple tasks because of a lack of technology literacy.

The United States as a nation has not ensured that the average citizen is keeping up with the ability to function in society by using technology. In one example from the public library sphere, a patron comes in wanting to use a public Internet access terminal provided by the library. The patron receives a guest pass or necessary credentials and goes over and signs on to the computer. They open Internet Explorer, and, in this example, Internet Explorer defaults to Google as a home page. The user immediately types www.hotmail .com into the Google search box. The patron's goal is to check his Hotmail e-mail, but he doesn't have the basic understanding that web addresses go into the address bar of a web browser and not into a search box. The user clicks on a "sponsored link" on the Google search results page instead of the correct search result, and suddenly he is on the wrong website and completely lost, unsure of why he is unable to access his email. The patron comes to the front desk to ask for help from the librarian. The librarian goes over to the computer, clicks once on the back button, then once on the correct Hotmail link, and walks away. In reality, the librarian should also stay and explain to the patron why typing the web address into the correct browser location is important. This is how libraries and librarians can help patrons to become more technology literate.

In another example, users may believe they need to register for a new e-mail account every time they visit Hotmail. Some users may type usernames (AND passwords!!) into the address bars and search bars of various websites. Patrons can spend in excess of 30 minutes trying to create a password that complies with a site's password rules and trying to navigate a CAPTCHA.

A **CAPTCHA**, short for "Completely Automated Public Turing test to tell Computers and Humans Apart," is a type of security question on a web form in which the user is asked to read and then type a series of visually scrambled letters or numbers. The letters and numbers are obscured enough that computers cannot read them, but humans should be able to successfully read them and type this information into a box. If the information typed matches the previously defined answer that the web form expects for that particular CAPTCHA, then the form is considered valid and is processed.

Some cases are even more severe. A few patrons may not know how to use a mouse at all or have a problem transferring from an external mouse to a touchpad on a laptop keyboard. Some patrons may not be able to locate the Backspace key.

To clear up one popular misconception immediately: These example patrons are not all 90-year-old senior citizens. The patrons who demonstrate technology illiteracy come from a variety of walks of life. It's very common to get middle-aged patrons trying to apply for jobs who have never had to fill out an online application before. Equally common are some shockingly young patrons from what the media likes to call the "technology generation," who need assistance with basic tasks such as loading and saving files to a thumb drive.

So why tell you all of this? Why preach about the dire state of science, technology, engineering, and math (STEM) abilities in this country? Because in several different ways, it affects how you do your job.

First, with regards to technology and equipment available to the public, when users report a problem, you have to make very sure that the problem is not really with the users themselves. This seems like a logical conclusion; we take for granted that since they're performing simple tasks like using a word processor that they must be getting them right and that any malfunctions must be the result of software or hardware set up on the machine. However, because your time is limited, you cannot take anything for granted. Observe the following scenario:

Librarian: How can I help you today?
Patron: My thumb drive won't work in your public computers. They seem awfully slow. Is there anything you can do?
Librarian: I'm sorry to hear that. Let me walk over there with you and we'll get it figured out together.
              (at the computer)
Librarian: Now show me what you were trying to do when you had the problem.
Patron: I stuck the thumb drive in like this, but Windows doesn't recognize it.
Librarian: You have it in backward.

Flipping the thumb drive around (it was the super-slim type that can fit in the USB port either way), the computer recognized the thumb drive right away.

The computer wasn't exceptionally slow. That was either a red herring or a mental manifestation of the user's frustration.

The quickest way to assess any situation is to not take anecdotes or second-hand information if at all possible. Observe what the patron is doing on the computer first-hand and offer them on-the-spot guidance to correct the issue. This will save you having to open a mental trouble ticket for the issue.

If you aren't able to verify the issue with the patron because they leave before you can talk to them, or you receive a second-hand report from another staff member, use the rule of two.

1. Verify quickly that the computer in question is working, but don't spend an exceptional amount of time trying to re-create the problem.
2. Wait. If another patron reports the same problem, then you can go after it with some aggression.

This is in no way saying that you shouldn't be proactive about reported technology problems with public-facing equipment. But you also have to be realistic and honest with yourself that a scribbled note reporting some vague trouble with a machine is going to be nearly impossible to track down if the machine appears to be acting correctly when you visit it. In that case, you will really need a patron to demonstrate the trouble as it happens if you have any hope of accurately re-creating and diagnosing the issue.

The other way that technology illiteracy can affect your work is during survey and public opinion time. This is something that you want to make sure and point out to your supervisor if he or she isn't already aware of it. John Q. Public really isn't qualified to unilaterally say that the computer setup in the library "is worthless," even though they'll be more than happy to tell you so on anonymous surveys and suggestion cards. The patron possibly tried to perform some task on the computers for which the patron was woefully unqualified, such as editing photos with no training or running a home-based business with no prior experience. Alternately, the patron might have been trying to do an incredibly specialized task for which the computer was woefully inadequate. As an example, two younger patrons complained that the speed of the computer they were using at the library couldn't keep up with the high-definition videogame that they were trying to play. The budget, of course, was too limited to purchase special high-power computers for their gaming use. That doesn't mean the computers we provided weren't just fine for everyday use.

Make sure that you don't put yourself in a position where your supervisor comes down on you with a notebook of complaints about technology, taking each and every one as the gospel truth and as a direct representation of your performance as an IT manager. This is, unfortunately, very easy for supervisors to do, especially if they don't really understand the technology. The common ground is that sometimes complaints like these are received about other library services, and so the supervisor should be able to relate to the fact that all comments need to be taken with a grain of salt. Help the supervisor to understand this.

Technology literacy is an ongoing problem for some patrons in public libraries. This lack of technology literacy among patrons will affect the way that you do your job. Because of this, you must learn to carefully evaluate the statements of a patron before jumping to conclusions about problems with technology in the library.

CHAPTER 16

Dealing with the Public 102: Managing Your Own Superhero Status

Though this theme is touched on throughout this book, one critical point of your job that you might not have considered is the appearance of your competence. After reading this book and after getting some practice, people are going to start noticing what you do. In fact, if you even appear competent in the field of IT, expect word to spread like wildfire that you know what you're talking about. All manner of people will suddenly start showing up at your desk with all kinds of questions. Some questions are easily solvable and directly concern the work you do at the library. A good example of this type of question is, "What button do I click on to find this book in the library catalog?" (Generally quick to solve and in line with library topics and services, so plus two points.) Some questions are a little further off the mark: for example, "How do I install the drivers for this printer?" It is a reference question, so plus one point, but not exactly in line with typically offered library services, so minus one point. Then there are the questions that are simply beyond your capacity as an IT person and a librarian: "Can you help me set up my new laptop?" (Way, way too much time and not specific enough.) "Can you help me write my résumé on the computer?" (Define the amount of help they need in advance or you might end up writing it for them.) "Can you help me install this coupon program on the computer so I can download them from the website?" (Adding bloatware requests should always be denied.) Finally, there are the questions that are so far out in left field that you end up with them just because no one else has any idea: "Can you help me modify my microwave oven into an Em-Drive like I've been hearing about in the news?" (Yikes.)

Other questions are a combination of all of the earlier categories and arise out of a fundamental misunderstanding of technology and the operations of computers. Perhaps you could throw a dash of paranoia in there for good measure. A patron might ask, "I've heard that the government includes a chip in all new computers that allows the NSA to spy on what you're doing through the built-in webcam on your computer. How can I keep them from doing this?" Creativity, but not sarcasm, is called for in this instance. Resist the urge to say, "Just unplug it and leave it unplugged," or, "Are you sure you're qualified to be operating that equipment in the first place?" Instead, a healthy dose of imagination, grounded in reality, can really make a person's day: "I'm not aware that the NSA is installing such chips, but if you are concerned, my suggestion would be to put a small piece of opaque tape over the webcam on your computer or close the shutter. This will prevent anyone from inadvertently viewing you while you use the machine."

Obviously, there were a host of things wrong with the patron's question, but the intention was good, and you have to take the intention and work with it to avoid offending the person.

The sheer volume of questions you'll get as a public-service IT person, let alone the content of those questions, may overwhelm you. From the people who expect that you'll solve every problem for free because their tax dollars pay your salary, to the people who are just genuinely confused about technology and don't know which questions to ask, to the weirdos who don't fit in any other category, you'll get them all.

That's why it is very, very important to have in place a procedure for how you are going to handle these questions as they arise. Specifically, what types of limits are you going to set to ensure that your time and liability are respected?

You could have a formal policy in place, rather than a procedure, but remember that policies are generally something that are put in place by the library board of trustees and require the library board's vote to amend or change. If something isn't working out with the rules you've set down, it's much easier to simply make the necessary changes in a procedure than have to wait for the Library Board to change it as a policy at the monthly meeting. On the other hand, having a policy does lend it somewhat more "clout" than a procedure. The best thing to do is to split the difference and have the Library Board recognize in writing that they are delegating the responsibility to your job title to make and enforce such procedures necessary for the effective handling of questions and operations of customer service as it concerns IT in the library.

This "Technology Assistance Procedures" document should touch on several different points. The first point is **time**. If a patron asks you a long series of questions or asks you to leave the desk and your customer service role to assist them at a computer, how long is too long to continue answering questions for them? If you've worked in a public library more than two days, you've already met the patron who will literally keep talking to you until you walk away. It doesn't matter if they've asked the same question twenty different ways or if they're making a circular argument; you're going to be responsible for concluding the transaction when you've hit your time limit. That's why it's important to know how much time you will spend with them in advance. The amount of time you spend will depend most directly on your staffing needs. This is critical if you are the only person managing the library at a given time. If you're the only one at the desk, your transaction time to help patrons away from the desk at their own computers may be zero. Or it may be only as long as it takes for the next customer to arrive. When there are two staff members, you may want to limit any transaction to 10 minutes so that one staff member isn't responsible for handling all of the other desk service for longer than that. Also, think about the wording you want to use when you have to end an over-time transaction. Do you want to state that you can help them again when you have a few minutes or simply tell them politely that their questions have gone beyond the amount of help that you are able to provide and that you won't be able to assist them further?

Second, **liability.** This one is extremely important. Think about the limits of what you are willing to do for a patron. This is especially relevant when patrons bring their own laptop or mobile device and want you to help to reconfigure it. If you take over the keyboard and mouse from the patron, you run the risk that the patron will return later and accuse you of causing problems with the device. Generally, you won't actually be responsible for this, but some patrons know so little about the functioning or malfunctioning of technology that what they're really looking for is someone to blame. It's sad but true. For this reason, some libraries have procedures that explicitly state that staff will not navigate the patron's computer for the patron. In other words, the librarian instructs patrons in a task, but the patrons will ultimately be responsible for executing the task on their personal machine. You can expect the patron to immediately say, "But I'm so bad at this, why don't you just do it?" At this point, don't hesitate to explain to them that you're limiting your liability. It doesn't hurt to tell them the truth, and many times they'll be better prepared to assist you after that explanation.

Also, are there limits to the *types* of work that you won't advise about? Some patrons will ask you questions that obviously carry a high degree of liability, such as: "How do I recover my Windows password?" or "How do I re-format my hard drive?" Liability is definitely a discussion you'll want to have with your supervisor, possibly with the Library Board and possibly with your organization's attorney.

Third, you want to spell out limits on the use of your public computers. Among the most common questions is: "The computer says I need administrator rights to install this program. Can you give those to me?" Though the final decision is up to you, your answer should be unequivocally "NO." Granting administrator rights on your machine for the purposes of installing a program not only sets a terrible precedent but also opens the machine up to a host of problems. The most common request involves the specialized "coupon" apps that must be installed in order to validate, download, and print coupons from various websites. Virtually all of these coupon apps ask for administrator rights, and you should not allow installations or any other functions that require extra administrator rights. This limits the potential damage to the machine, as well as limits the possibility that someone could inadvertently lift an administrator password, which means the person could conceivably log in to the machine as an administrator, at which point he or she would have complete configuration control over the computer and could potentially wreak havoc. In addition, it prevents the general desk staff from having to know the administrator credentials. While the credentials can't be entirely secret, it's best if there's a first line of defense that prevents other staff from installing all manner of bloatware to the machines in the library.

Bloatware is a name for programs installed on a computer that are unnecessary and serve to eat up the system resources of the computer, which results in a slow machine. A good example is coupon programs. Each couponing website has a different piece of software that has to be downloaded in order to validate coupons. After visiting several of these websites, the computer will have several pieces of software installed and running on the computer, which effectively serve no purpose and only slow the computer down.

Fourth, you should address when to contact the IT person. You have other roles and responsibilities besides IT work. Because of that, you can't be jumping up from your desk every 10 seconds to answer a patron's question simply because other staff members don't want to give it the "old college try." Encourage staff, especially those who are hesitant about technology, to use what they do know or what you have taught them to try and come up with an answer for the patron. For example, though a staff member may not know the release date of Office 2016, you have taught them how to use Google, and Google will provide the answer. Explain that an IT question is no different from any other reference question, except that it involves a computer. Try to set some ground rules and limits so that staff members at least attempt to find a solution before coming to you for help. Even the most well-intentioned staff will, if unguided, fall into a routine of leaning more and more heavily on you as the IT guru to answer IT questions. You need to stake out your territory and your own limits so that you can be an effective, productive employee as well.

It may seem like all of these restrictions simply harm the patron and limit what we are allowed to do for them. On the contrary, it is to ensure equitable service among all patrons and to ensure that a patron with an exceptionally long or complex IT question does not monopolize staff to the detriment of the library or other patrons. Very few patrons with an IT question come with the intention of monopolizing anything. But IT questions especially are prone to this happening because

1. they are complicated and often confusing;
2. the patron is genuinely curious for more details about the solution; and
3. the requests may be for a service that the library simply cannot provide.

Unfortunately, there are a few patrons who will treat the library and its staff like a "for free" IT Shop, as opposed to the local computer shop down the road that charges $50 an hour just to look at your machine. As you well know, staffing and time restrictions don't allow for the library to function in this capacity. Having an effective document that outlines what you can and will and cannot and will not do for patrons in the realm of IT is an important first step.

An effective document that informs patrons and staff of the types and limits on IT services that the library provides is essential for maintaining quality customer service for all patrons and for reasonably limiting the flow of IT questions that come across your desk.

CHAPTER 17

Conclusion

So we've come to the end of this book. If there's one conclusion that you can draw immediately, it's that IT work is not as simple as it appears, even in a setting like a small public library. It is nuanced, complex, and ever-changing; unlike any other job within the library sphere.

But despite the headaches and occasional indigestion it may cause, IT is critically important in the modern library. At its most basic, the integrated library system requires a stable IT infrastructure. Book transactions such as checkouts would not occur if the network or computers were not there to support the ILS program.

Many of the "clerical tasks" are now done via computer. Informative signs, electronic slide shows, pamphlets, board reports, and all manner of other documents are created on computer and stored there.

From the staff perspective, the computer serves as the ultimate research tool. From Googling the weather for a patron to looking up the next book in a book series to checking Amazon for a hard-to-find book, the IT department provides the connection to the world that is required to fulfill the modern expectation of library services.

Then there's the patron side of things. There will be days when you will be tempted to throw up your hands and say, "Why do I even bother?" when it comes to providing public computers and other electronic resources for patrons. You may even have doubts in your own mind about whether providing computers and piles of electronic databases and resources is really in line with the traditional mission of a public library. This author has had those days.

Understand, however, that there is no more important role to fill for a library than that of a great equalizer. A library does not simply provide resources such as books and computers; it levels the playing field among all social classes and economic classes and by its existence eliminates barriers such as income, race, or disability. It's easy to forget that not everyone can afford an Internet connection, a computer, or even a book. A library ensures *equitable access to information*, and information remains the most important resource of all.

Because of this, it is our duty as librarians to ensure equitable access to information in whatever format the information is provided. More and more information, from news headlines to stock quotes to sports scores to medical knowledge is provided on the Internet. Further, many if not most major employers are now requiring online applications for job seekers. Ensuring equitable access to information necessitates that we defend the idea of public computers and Internet (as well as wireless Internet) in the public library.

Your role as a librarian and as an IT professional is a critically important link between the two worlds of traditional print books and modern information sources such as the Internet. You alone are uniquely qualified to speak on how the library is serving both sets of needs and continuing to ensure equality well into the 21st century. Technology belongs in the public library, and it is here to stay. Hopefully, this book has provided some assistance as you continue to manage IT in your public library. You're doing exceptionally important work.

GLOSSARY

Amperes—colloquially called "amps," they are the actual measure of electrical current. Amperes determine how much work a flow of electricity can perform. Electrical circuits in buildings can only provide a limited number of amperes before circuit breakers automatically trip, stopping the flow of electricity.

Basic Input/Output System (BIOS)—a chip located on the motherboard, which contains programming that controls the very first moments of a computer's boot cycle and controls some basic hardware functions while the computer is in operation.

Beep Codes—diagnostic or error codes presented in the form of a series of beeps from a computer's internal speaker. Beep codes are intended to relay hardware or boot problems reported by the computer's BIOS.

Bezel—a trim piece that sticks out of the front of the case to provide a "finished" look to drive bays and other modular computer components.

Bloatware—is a name for programs installed on a computer that are unnecessary and serve to eat up the system resources of the computer, which results in a slow machine.

Blue Screen of Death—appears when the core routines of the Windows operating system don't know how to handle an error, and so Windows stops the operating system program altogether (a fatal error). This will either trigger an automatic reboot or present a blue screen with information on the cause of the crash.

Boot Disk—a removable disk such as a CD, from which the computer can automatically operate when the machine is started; if a boot disk is present, the computer will ignore the operating system on the primary hard drive and instead load an operating system from the boot disk.

Boot Sector—a special reserved area of a computer's primary hard disk drive that contains information critical to continuing the boot process after control is handed off from the computer's BIOS.

Booting—the process by which a computer comes to life and literally "pulls itself up by its bootstraps," going from a dead piece of silicon and metal to loading instructions and software such that, within a minute or two, the system is completely ready to use.

Bricking—a term to describe making your computer permanently unusable. One of the most common ways of accomplishing this is through a failed BIOS firmware update.

CAPTCHA—short for "Completely Automated Public Turing test to tell Computers and Humans Apart," it is a type of security question on a web form in which the user is asked to read and then type a series of visually scrambled letters or numbers. The letters and numbers are obscured enough that computers cannot read them, but humans should be able to successfully read them and type this information into a box. If the information typed matches the previously defined answer that the web form expects for that particular CAPTCHA, then the form is considered valid and is processed.

Chips—also known as integrated circuits. They are a package that contains the electronics that run the modern computer.

Chipset—a collection of integrated circuits ("chips") on a computer motherboard that work together.

Circuit Breakers—designed to automatically shut off electricity if the amperes demanded by a particular circuit exceeds what the circuit is able to provide.

Client—a standard computer on a network that obtains resources from a server, such as file shares and network credential authentication.

Cold Boot—completely powering off a computer, draining any remaining power, letting it sit, and then repowering the computer.

Complementary Metal Oxide Semiconductor (CMOS)—stores some basic settings for how the computer should behave at the hardware level.

Control Panel—a utility in the Windows operating system that allows you to control many of the settings of your computer.

Create a Recovery Drive—a Windows program that allows the user to create a bootable USB drive with critical system restoration information. In the event of a failure of the Windows operating system, this may allow the user to successfully recover it to a useable state.

Credentials—usernames and passwords.

Defragmentation—a process whereby a computer places all of the data belonging to a particular file close together, which speeds up access to that file.

Demarcation—the point at which one network begins and another ends; the term usually indicates a change in networking media. Demarcation points allow two disparate networks to be connected.

Disk Cleanup—a Windows operating system utility that allows the user to clean out various stores of temporary and other files on a computer, freeing up disk space.

Disk Defragmenter—a Windows operating system utility that allows the user to automatically rearrange file parts on a hard disk drive, so that parts belonging to the same file are close together, which reduces the time needed to load each file from disk.

DNS Address—the IP address of the DNS server that machines on the network use to translate human-readable device names into corresponding IP addresses.

Domain Name Server (DNS)—a server that accepts human-readable device names and sends back the appropriate corresponding IP address for the name. All computers that communicate with the Internet communicate with a DNS server in order to translate web addresses into IP addresses.

Drivers—special software that allows your computer operating system to communicate with the hardware components attached to the computer.

Dynamic Host Control Protocol (DHCP)—a protocol that allows a network device, such as a router or server, to dynamically assign IP addresses to various networking devices upon request by the devices. The opposite of static IP addresses.

Encryption—the process of mathematically re-coding the contents of a file based on a formula. Encryption operates by taking an input string of characters (known as a "key") and using that key to calculate what the new value of each bit in the file should be.

Error Logs—records kept by the operating system about various problems encountered, including the type and severity of the error and the date and time that it occurred.

Ethernet—the most commonly used networking standard, which sets things like how data is transmitted and how the network should be physically assembled.

Event Viewer—a Microsoft Windows operating system program used to help review logs.

Expansion Cards—smaller boards that plug into the motherboard. Not as common as they were in the past, as more functions are now integrated directly into the motherboard circuitry.

Facet Tool—also known as a "drill-down" tool, this allows a user to narrow his or her search by checking boxes to represent included categories for the search. After enough categories are added, only a few products or materials remain, which fit into all of the required categories.

Fat Client—the opposite of a thin client, it is simply another way of referring to a "full-featured" desktop computer that is a client of a server on a network. Fat clients can generally operate independently of the server if necessary.

Firewall—a network device that prevents malicious data from reaching the local network from the Internet.

Flash Drive or Thumb Drive—a small, rectangular storage device that plugs into an USB port and is used in the same way as a traditional disk drive. Files can be saved to and opened directly from a flash drive.

Font—a particular visual style applied to text, which changes its appearance.

Gateway Address—the IP address that networking equipment and attached devices such as computers use to communicate with a higher-level network (such as the Internet). Often this IP address is the address of the network's router or firewall.

Gigabyte (GB)—a measurement of a quantity of data; it is approximately 1,000 megabytes.

Graphical User Interface (GUI)—allows users to interact with the computer using graphics, such as double-clicking icons to open a program.

Ground—also called earth, it is an alternate path for electricity to take in the event of a short or other problem that causes unintended parts of a device to become electrically live. For example, a proper ground would prevent a computer case from presenting a shock hazard in the event of a short within the computer that made the case electrically live.

Hard Disk Drive (HDD)—located inside your computer, it is the primary storage area for data and files on your computer, which remain even when the machine is powered off.

Hub—an obsolete piece of networking equipment that generally preceded the network switch. Hubs did not "learn" about which devices were connected to each of their ports, and as a result simply repeated all traffic to every attached machine. This tended to cause unneeded network congestion and is slower than the modern network switch.

Information Literacy—this means that an individual is able to quickly recognize the information that they need and is able to effectively and efficiently retrieve that credible information from an appropriate source.

InfraRecorder—free program for burning various downloaded ISOs to CDs or DVDs.

Integrated Library System (ILS)—the software that controls a library's day-to-day functioning. The software records check-in and checkout of materials, patron data such as names and phone numbers, and fines and fees, among other functions. It also provides a web-based catalog for public use.

Internet Protocol (IP) Address—a numerical address assigned to each device on a network that allows for communication between devices. These addresses can be changed.

IP Conflicts—a situation when two or more devices on a network have exactly the same IP address. This is often a problem with static IP addressing because mistakes are made and addresses are assigned that already are in use. DHCP automatically avoids creating IP conflicts.

IPv4—the IP address standard for many years, it is presented in the form aaa.bbb.ccc.ddd. It is still in general use, especially on private local networks.

IPv6—superseded IPv4 as the IP address standard because, quite simply, the world ran out of usable IPv4 addresses. It is used on large networks and some newer small local networks. At this time, it is not necessary to use IPv6 unless you have a specific need for it.

ISO—(pronounced ICE-O) a bit-by-bit data copy of a disk designed to be burned directly onto a blank CD or DVD.

Kernel Panic—a programming routine triggered when an operating system cannot continue due to a major hardware or software error. Generally, a kernel panic routine will cause error logs to be written and cause the error information to be dumped to the screen, as is the case with the infamous "blue screen of death." A kernel panic may or may not initiate an automatic reboot of the computer.

Link Lights—lights on a port that indicate that the cable is correctly connected to equipment on both ends of the cable.

Logs—automatic records kept by the computer of various events that occur in the operating system. Users can review these log files to determine when certain events occurred within the system, which helps track down problems.

MAC Address—a unique identifying number that is permanently assigned to each Network Interface Card. This number allows identification of a device by other network equipment, such as network switches.

Mail-Merge database—a database file generally constructed in Microsoft Access, which contains names and contact information.

Mbps and Gbps—short for Megabits per second and Gigabits per second, they are measures of the speed at which data is transmitted from one piece of equipment to another. 1 Gbps is approximately equal to 1,000 Mbps.

Media Access Control Address (MAC Address)—a permanent address assigned to each network card that is made up of a combination of a number assigned to the manufacturer and a number that varies with each Network Interface Card.

Megabyte (MB)—a measurement of a quantity of data, approximately 1,000,000 bytes.

Metadata—this is information about information. A common example is "tagging" a post on the Internet with key words to make it more searchable and accessible, such as Twitter's hashtags.

Memory Leak—caused when a running computer program fails to free all of the memory that it reserved while it was in use. This reduces the remaining available memory for other programs because the operating system will refuse to reassign memory that it believes to be in use.

Memory Stick—also called a memory module or RAM stick, it is a small rectangular circuit board centrally located on the motherboard of the computer that plugs in perpendicular. It contains several RAM chips that provide the computer with some amount of memory (common values today are 2 GB and 4 GB).

Microsoft Updates—patches and other software enhancements released by Microsoft and intended for Microsoft products, such as the Windows operating system and Microsoft Office. Windows has a built-in utility to check for these updates.

Modem—a device that, traditionally, allowed the user to communicate between computers over a phone line. Now the term is used to represent any translating device used to communicate with a higher-level network, such as a cable modem allowing a local network to connect to the Internet.

Motherboard—main circuit board in the computer that contains the processor and slots for memory and expansion cards. In conjunction with the processor, this board controls the functioning of the computer.

Natural Language Search—a search engine's ability to take a phrase written in the form a human being would speak and algorithmically turn that into an internal search phrase and use it to return appropriate, relevant results.

Network Interface Card (NIC)—hardware in a computer or other device that allows it to connect to a local network. This may be built directly into the motherboard of a computer.

Network Map—a graphical representation of the layout of a computer network.

Network Ports—sockets on networking equipment to which Ethernet patch cables are attached. Also refers to the end-user Ethernet sockets set in walls that deliver network connections from the networking equipment to the user.

Network Rack—a vertical steel rack to which various pieces of networking equipment are attached.

Network Switch—a network device that "learns" which computers or other devices are attached to its network ports. Then, given a packet of data from the router that is bound for a specific computer or other device, it can very quickly deliver that data to the right port.

Open Source—a term meaning that the programming code that makes up the software is available for anyone to inspect and modify.

Opera—a brand name of a web browsing program, just like Internet Explorer and Firefox. Opera is available for free download and use at www.opera.com.

Packets—chunks of data transmitted over a network.

Patch Cable—short cables used to connect networking devices to each other and to connect networking devices to a patch panel.

Patch Panel Map—a graphical representation of which patch panel port connects to each network port located throughout the building.

Patch Panels—a board of network ports on the network rack that act as a pass through to quickly connect networking equipment to Ethernet cables that run all over the building.

Patron Authentication Software—allows librarians to automatically control who is allowed to access library computers. Usually a computer user will have to enter his or her library card number in order to gain access to a public computer.

Persistent State Software—software that allows the administrator to freeze a computer in a particular state such that, when the computer is restarted, it acts exactly as it did when it was first set up. Any changes made to the computer during a session with active persistent state software are erased.

Polling—a process by which the network devices learn about themselves and other devices to which they are attached. One common example is a network switch communicating with each of its ports in turn to determine what device is attached.

Port—a female connector located on a piece of equipment. It accepts the male connectors from a particular type of cable.

Port Gender—the practice of identifying ports and plugs as either male or female. It is adopted from more traditional mammalian anatomy terms. A plug with prongs or pins is known as a male connector. A port or socket designed to receive one of these connectors with pins is known as a female connector.

Power Cycle—the process of turning off a piece of equipment (such as a computer), removing power sources, and draining remaining power, then reapplying a power source and restarting the machine.

Power on Self Test (POST)—low-level checks on the functioning of computer hardware before the boot process continues when memory is verified and tested, expansion cards (if any) are tested, various chip components such as Ethernet and video are tested, and drives, such as the hard disk drive, are detected.

Power over Ethernet (PoE)—system whereby a networking device can use a standard Ethernet cable to provide the voltage necessary to operate a connected device, not just to transmit the data. PoE is often used with wireless access points because these devices are usually in locations where electrical outlets are not practical.

Processor Architectures—differences in the way that computer processors function. Programs using a processor with a particular architecture must generally be written to run on it. For example, programs written for an ×64 processor, also called 64-bit programs, may not work with an older computer with an ×86 (32-bit) processor architecture.

Rack Unit—unit of measurement for the height of networking equipment. One rack unit (RU) is approximately 1.75" high.

Random Access Memory—also called RAM, or just memory, it is temporary storage space for program data that can be written and retrieved quickly by the computer, much faster than retrieving information off the hard drive. Random access memory is erased when the computer is turned off.

Release Notes—a document provided by a company that tells you about enhancements provided by a particular software patch or upgrade.

Request for Bids (RFB)—traditionally means a request for companies to send bids for goods such as new computers. The term's use may vary by organization.

Request for proposals (RFP)—traditionally means a request for companies to send proposals for services such as web design. The term's use may vary by organization.

Restart or Warm Boot—a repeat of the start-up sequence without physically removing power to the device.

Router—a networking device that sorts data on a network and routes it, for example, to the correct computer. A common application is to allow a large number of computers to share and communicate with a higher-level network, such as an Internet connection.

Safe Mode—a Windows utility that allows one to gain control of Windows when normal start-up fails. Once in safe mode, the user can determine what is wrong with Windows and fix it to restore normal operation.

SD Card—a flat, nearly square chip that slides into a compatible SD card slot on your computer. It is a storage device, so files can be written to and read from a SD card in the same way as a flash drive. SD cards are common in digital cameras and mobile phones. They come in a variety of sizes.

Servers—a specialized computer on a network specifically designed to provide resources to other machines, such as file sharing and network credential authentication.

Standard—a declared manner in which all devices of a particular type must operate so that cables, equipment, and data transmission schemes are compatible with one another across all vendors.

Static Addressing (IP)—the opposite of DHCP addressing. Each device on the network, such as a computer, is assigned a semi-permanent IP address that the device will always use when communicating with the network. The address does not change unless it is manually changed on the device itself.

Subnet Mask—a method of mathematically interpreting IP addresses.

Subnets—dividing a single network into logically separate networks by isolating IP address pools from one another. For example, on an IPv4 network, 10.10.31.ddd and 10.10.32.ddd would be on logically separate subnets and unable to communicate with one another.

Technology Literacy—the ability to interact with electronic devices in a logical manner that allows the user to quickly learn and manipulate the technology. It allows the user to find common ground to perform essential functions on a device even if they have never seen or used that type of technology before.

Temporary Files—files used by programs on a temporary basis. When a program needs to temporarily store data, it creates files on the computer hard drive and parks the data in those files.

Thin Client—a computer that relies more heavily on a server for direction than a typical computer; in some instances, a thin client must be provided with an operating system by the server each time it is turned on.

Third-Party Updates—in this book, refers to updates that are not either Microsoft updates or antivirus updates. Third-party updates include such things as Adobe Flash Player and the Java Runtime Environment (JRE).

Thumbscrews—similar to regular computer case screws, but with exceptionally oversized screw heads that generally allow the screws to be operated using only one's thumbs.

Tripping—occurs when a circuit breaker automatically shuts off the flow of electricity due to overloading a circuit.

Unified Extensible Firmware Interface (UEFI)—a successor to traditional computer BIOS, it allows the operator to control more setup functions of the computer prior to launching the operating system.

Uninterruptible Power Supply (UPS)—a network device that filters incoming electricity so that high and low voltages do not adversely affect networking equipment. The device can also provide power for equipment in the event of a complete electricity outage.

Update—a fix or correction to software, such as Microsoft Office, which is issued after the product is released.

Uplinking—connecting one network switch to another so that they may communicate, effectively, as one larger switch. Modern network switches do this automatically if connected.

Virtual Desktop—in thin client computing, a virtual desktop is a mini-operating system that allows the user to interact with the server in a familiar environment (such as Windows) while on the client, when really the server is providing almost all of the processing.

Virtual Local Area Network (VLAN)—allows a network switch to service two separate networks or subnets at the same time.

Volts—a measure of electrical pressure, it indicates how much resistance the electricity can overcome. With higher voltages, electricity can be convinced to jump through the air, such as with static electricity and lightning. Electricity can pass through human skin at a relatively low voltage.

Wireless Access Point—a device that provides a doorway into an existing network for wireless devices. Unlike a wireless router, wireless access points cannot function independently; they rely on an existing network router and DNS server to manage the flow of information to and from wireless devices.

Wireless Router—a networking device that creates a wireless subnetwork. It connects and manages the data of multiple wireless clients (such as laptops) at the same time. A complete network can be created with nothing more than an Internet connection and a wireless router.

INDEX

Note: Page numbers followed by t indicate a table. Italicized page numbers indicate a figure.

ABOUT THE AUTHOR

CHRISTOPHER D. BROWN holds a master's degree in information science and learning technologies with an emphasis in library science from the University of Missouri–Columbia and has worked for more than eight years in public libraries as an IT professional. He believes in the coming singularity between public library services and publicly accessible technology and believes that technology has the power to change lives. Mr. Brown lives with his wife and two children in Pella, Iowa. Visit him on the web at youreitsoloit.com.